HD6276.C32 M37 19. W9-CKC-179

Marquardt, Richard.

Enter at your own risk :
Canadian youth and the
1998.

1999 03 08

A-7

Enter at Your Own Risk

with photos by Vincenzo Pietropaolo

Enter at Your Own Risk: Canadian Youth and the Labour Market

130101
AEX 7542

Richard Marquardt

SIR SANDFORD FLEMING
COLLEGE
BREALEY LIBRARY
APR 1 3 1999
PETERBOROUGH

BETWEEN THE LINES
TORONTO, CANADA

Enter at Your Own Risk: Canadian Youth and the Labour Market
© Richard Marquardt, 1998

All rights reserved. No part of this publication may be photocopied, reproduced, stored in a retrieval system, or transmitted in any form or by any means, electronic, mechanical, recording, or otherwise, without the written permission of Between the Lines, or CANCOPY (photo-copying only), 6 Adelaide Street East, Suite 900, Toronto, Ontario, M5C 1H6.

Between the Lines gratefully acknowledges financial assistance for our publishing activities from the Ontario Arts Council, The Canada Council for the Arts, and the Government of Canada through the Book Publishing Industry Development Program.

Every reasonable effort has been made to find copyright holders. The publisher would be pleased to have any errors or omissions brought to its attention.

Canadian Cataloguing in Publication Data

Marquardt, Richard
        Enter at your own risk

Includes bibliographical references and index.
ISBN 1-896357-19-9

1. Youth — Employment — Canada. 2. Labour market — Canada.
3. Youth — Canada. 4. Unemployment — Canada. I. Title.

HD6276.C32M37 1998   331.3'4'0971   C98-932049-9

Photos: Vincenzo Pietropaolo
Cover Design: Stray Toaster
Interior Design: Steve Izma
Cover Photo: Gregory Nixon

SIR SANDFORD FLEMING
COLLEGE
BREALEY LIBRARY

APR 1 3 1999

PETERBOROUGH

Printed in Canada by Transcontinental

1 2 3 4 5 6 7 8 9 10   05 04 03 02 01 00 99 98

Between the Lines
720 Bathurst Street, #404, Toronto, Ontario, M5S 2R4, Canada
(416) 535-9914   btlbooks@web.net

Contents

Preface vii

1 "It Has Galvanized Everybody . . ." 1

2 Coming of Age in Canada: 1850-1945 13

3 From Golden Age to Risk Society: The Postwar World 37

4 Education and Changing Aspirations 53

5 Making Their Way: The Labour-Market Experience 71

6 Changing Patterns: Earnings, Incomes, and Personal Life 89

7 Policy Responses to Labour-Market Problems 109

8 Conclusion: Social Solutions and Alternative Approaches 137

Notes 145

For Sarah and James

Preface

*T*his book had its origins in an academic paper I undertook in 1994 as a student at Queen's University's School of Policy Studies. I had returned to school in middle age, at the same time as my own daughter and son were making their way through university and facing uncertain prospects in the labour market. I had conspired with them to reinforce the mainstream, middle-class Canadian idea that they were doing the right thing — continuing their education to complete some form of postsecondary degree or diploma at a university or college. As a child of the sixties, I did not worry at first about their choice of a field of study. If pressed to give them advice, I fell back on the old stand-by: "Study what interests you. You only get to have one life, so there is no point in wasting it on studies and a career that hold no interest for you." That's what I had done, and it had worked for me, at least to that point in my life.

But, I worried, was it good advice? The early 1990s were bleak times. My own motives for further studies were mixed. I had worked most of my career in the field of international co-operation, an industry in decline due to cuts in government spending. I thought it would be prudent to retool for an uncertain future, but I also looked forward to relief from the stresses of a pressured workplace and the opportunity to research and think about what was happening to our society. After years of focusing on the problems of other countries, I thought it was time to pay attention to my own. Why had so many small towns in Eastern Ontario been suddenly deindustrialized? Why was it so difficult to make a living on a family farm? What were the prospects for the million-plus Canadians who were unemployed? I believed the Queen's program offered the opportunity to delve into these and similar questions with some expert assistance, and I was not disappointed.

In my second year I was required to begin work on an extended piece of research on a public-policy issue. I chose to work on the problems of youth in the labour market. Apart from the dim prospects faced by many middle-aged people like myself, it was the subject closest to home. By choosing it, however, I was soon forced to shift my focus away from the problems faced by my own children to the wide range of conditions and dilemmas faced by an entire generation. I found that the issue changed shape, became more complex.

On one level, the level on which I first approached it, it was a middle-class issue. Young people and their parents worried about the prospects even for well-educated youth. But there was another level that I had not paid much attention to: the rapid deterioration of labour-market conditions for those without postsecondary education. Young people who grew up in low-income families that could not afford to pay rising education costs, or who for any reason did not complete a high-school diploma and undertake some kind of postsecondary education, risked a future of poverty and marginalization. Moreover, they were easily branded as the authors of their own misfortune for not going further in school. Layered over this basic divide were differences based on gender, race, and ethnicity and on the regions they lived in. It took me a long time to sort through all of this complexity, to do justice to the genuine concerns of those who are relatively advantaged, and yet to focus on the larger problem of deep social divisions emerging in Canada through the lives of our young people.

I was fortunate to have Judith Maxwell as my academic adviser in this work. She encouraged me to take on the issue and was generous with her time and assistance. After completing the academic project at the School of Policy Studies in 1995, I expected to let go of the issue and return to my world of international co-operation. Instead, over the next three years, and to my surprise, I found myself working on a series of projects on different aspects of the problems of youth in the labour market. Each of these studies allowed me to broaden my understanding of the issues in different ways and brought me into contact with people who were grappling in their professional work with the problems of youth.

For assistance beyond the call of duty on one or more of these projects I would like to thank in particular Gordon Betcherman, Norm Leckie, Patrice de Broucker, Graham Lowe, Doug Giddings, Louise Boyer, and Jeff Frank.

Harvey Krahn gave me generous assistance and encouragement several times over the past few years. He also reviewed the manuscript of this book, as did Mercedes Steedman, as well as Jamie Swift and Ruth Bradley-St-Cyr of Between the Lines. Craig Heron reviewed the historical material. Each of these people made a valuable contribution to the final version, and Robert Clarke's deft and intelligent editing improved every page. As custom demands, I must take responsibility for all remaining errors and deficiencies.

A special thanks goes to Ivonne Mellozzi and Jacqueline Hallstead, both interns at Between The Lines, who added their enthusiasm and expertise to editing and marketing the book, respectively. We wish them well in their careers.

As a part of my research for this book I conducted intensive interviews with several young people who were in various stages of making the transition from youthful dependence to adult independence. As the final form of the book took shape, however, I decided to use only a small part of this material. I am grateful to those who gave me their time. Whether their stories appear here or not, they helped to ground me in the real world of their lives, beyond the abstraction of statistics and trends.

My son, James, was one of them. He also read an early draft of the manuscript and reminded me that the book should not be discouraging. Both he and my daughter, Sarah, have continued to be my inspirations.

My wife, Kate McLaren, helped to disentangle countless knots that I encountered. I thank her for all of the loving support — intellectual, moral, and material — that she gave me while I worked on this book.

Richard Marquardt
Ottawa, Ontario
October, 1998

1 "It Has Galvanized Everybody . . ."

We don't have to look far to find young Canadians who are venturing into the labour market. They are in our families, our neighbourhoods, our circles of friends. You might be one yourself. It is clear that many youth are having a difficult time in the Canadian labour market today. Still, very few think of themselves as victims. Almost any chance encounter with someone in their twenties provides a story that shows the complex relationship between young people's hopes and ambitions and the opportunities available to them. Here are two stories of my own.

><><

In the summer of 1997 my car broke down in the countryside a hundred miles west of Ottawa. The local garage couldn't solve the problem, so I had to have the car towed to Ottawa. On the two-hour drive the young tow-truck driver told me his story.

Darrell had started work after graduating from high school in Bancroft, Ontario. His family didn't have a lot of money, and he had never considered the possibility of going on to university or a community college. A generation earlier a young man like Darrell might have gone to Oshawa for a job at the GM plant. Darrell went to Toronto, where he

1

worked as a bricklayer's assistant for a few years. Eventually he realized he would need to have more than a high-school diploma if he were ever going to have a good job with a decent income. Hearing that there were lots of jobs in the computer field, he registered for the computer technician's course at Sir Sanford Fleming College in Peterborough. It was the accelerated, one-year program; the tuition was $5,000. He held down two part-time jobs during the year to pay his way, but still managed to complete the course successfully.

After graduating Darrell applied to over one hundred potential employers, receiving only a handful of replies and not a single interview. Disappointed, he felt he had been misled about the job opportunities in his field. He returned to Bancroft, where he started a small computer consulting business. He helped people with the set-up and repair of their systems. Darrell also had a lot of practical skills in auto mechanics and construction, but no formal qualifications in those fields. He found contract work doing renovations and building additions on homes in the Bancroft area. His knowledge of auto mechanics — plus, no doubt, his positive attitude and strong work ethic — got him casual work at the garage, where his main job was driving the tow-truck. At the time he told his story to me, he had three occupations: computer consultant, home renovator, and tow-truck driver. "You need to have a lot of different skills if you're going to live in a place like Bancroft," he told me.

>o<

I had met Christine a few months earlier at Oxfam-Canada's head office in Ottawa, where she was keeping the record of a workshop I was attending. During a break I asked her about her job. She told me she was a volunteer. At the time she had been working at the international aid agency's national office for no pay for three months, full-time — forty hours a week. She had organized Oxfam's archives, set up an electronic data base, and was working with staff on the preparation of a funding proposal to the Canadian International Development Agency (CIDA).

To Christine, this was not simply an altruistic donation of time to a good cause; it was the first step on her chosen career in international development. She had graduated from the University of Calgary in spring 1996 and moved to Ottawa that fall. "Ottawa is the main centre in Canada for international development organizations," she told me, "so when I finished my studies I came here to see what I could find." She knew no one in Ottawa; she had neither personal nor professional contacts. She had savings from her student job in Calgary — working at Wendy's — to keep her going for several months, if necessary.

When I first spoke to her in February 1997, Christine had not yet found the part-time job she was looking for. She had given her name to a private employment agency and paid up front for help in finding a job, possibly just a regular, minimum-wage restaurant job somewhere in town. She also spent time circulating her resumé to restaurants in Ottawa. She went to the local Human Resource Centre once, but they had no information on the kind of job she was looking for. "I've been telling myself I will have to start looking more seriously," she told me. "I can't last many more months without an income of some kind. But I have been learning and enjoying the work here, so I have put off looking."

Christine said she would have done better to take a minor in development studies instead of Canadian studies at university. She believed that would have prepared her better for what she wanted to do now. But it seems unlikely that it would have made any difference in her search for a regular job in the field. Around the same time Oxfam's Halifax office had a volunteer who held a Master's degree in development studies, and he had also had no luck finding work in his chosen field. Like Christine, he couldn't even find a minimum-wage job to keep him going. He had applied for a job as a telemarketer, but didn't get it.

A generation earlier, a young sociology graduate with Christine's desire to work in international development might have started out as a volunteer for an aid agency, such as CUSO or WUSC, which sent Canadians overseas to work in Africa, Asia, or Latin America, perhaps to participate in community development projects. With this experience as a base, the volunteer might have then, after further training, gone into a professional specialty — in demography, rural sociology, or urban planning, for example — and gone on to work with a United Nations agency, a Canadian government body, or a non-governmental organization (NGO), such as Oxfam. By the mid-1990s, volunteering overseas itself demanded professional qualifications and experience, while career jobs in development agencies were in decline due to public-sector funding cutbacks.

Christine had little prospect of a job opening up with Oxfam, but she didn't expect one. She was grateful for the opportunity to gain experience and have an entrée to the network of people and organizations in the field. She was determined to pursue this path until she achieved her goal, which was to have a career in international development. When I asked her why she was so determined to work in that field she looked a little embarrassed. "Apologies for the cliché," she said, "but I couldn't spend my life working at a job just for the income. I want the world to be a better place for my having been here."

>o<

Like most stories of young people, those of Darrell and Christine are in some ways typical and in other ways extraordinary. Darrell's story highlights the situation of youth in small towns and rural areas of the country, where the prospects are dim and getting worse. It also illustrates what can happen if young people get poor labour-market information when they are making critical decisions about education choices. Christine's story relates the difficulties experienced by many university and college graduates who are trying to get started in career jobs. Finally, both stories reflect something of the resilience and optimism of young people as they come to grips with today's economic conditions.

For balance, I might have added a story of someone who made an easy and successful transition from school to work. For example, I read a story in *The Globe and Mail* about a young man who was still working on his MBA at the University of Toronto but was already employed at BMW. The accompanying photograph showed him pulling out of the company parking lot in his new convertible. There are indeed stories like that one, too. In this book you will also read about young people who seem to be doing well, and who they are.

>o<

The plight of large numbers of youth is no secret. "It has galvanized everybody," cabinet minister Sergio Marchi told a reporter the day after the 1997 federal election. "It has galvanized their parents, their grandparents, their uncles, their aunts."[1] He was talking about youth unemployment, the hottest election issue that year. Other major issues — the environment, free trade, the crisis in Canada's military — had stirred not a ripple in the campaign, but everyone, it seemed, was anxious about the predicament of young people trying to get started in the labour market. At the time of the election the unemployment rate for youth aged fifteen to twenty-four was 16.7 per cent, compared to 9.6 per cent for the workforce as a whole. The rates were even higher in those parts of the country — Quebec and the Atlantic region — with chronic unemployment problems. Over four hundred thousand young people in the country as a whole were actively looking for work.

The problem, though, was not only unemployment but also the kind of work available. Much of it was low-paying, part-time, or temporary, jobs that had little or nothing to do with the aspirations or education of young people. These jobs may have been alright for students, working temporarily to get themselves through school, but many youth with university degrees or college diplomas were working as cashiers, sales clerks, telemarketers, or security guards. Other young people with only a high-school diploma or less had to get in line behind the better-educated for the chance to be a waiter or a switchboard operator.

Parents and relatives worry when their children are still living at home in their late twenties with no prospect of making the transition to adult independence because of low pay and insecure employment. Youth themselves feel anxiety when they face risky decisions about investing time and money in further education. Is it a good idea to spend three or four years amassing a debt of $25,000 or more to obtain a postsecondary qualification? This week they may hear that there are already too many lawyers, dentists, or MBAs. Next week they may hear about a big demand for systems analysts and computer programmers, but will that still be the case by the time they graduate? On the other hand, for job seekers without some kind of postsecondary qualification the prospects are bleak.

Some blame the baby-boom generation. Now in mid-life, the baby-boomers seem to occupy all of the good jobs — the secure, well-paying, career jobs that are so hard to find. True, many middle-aged people have lost their jobs in the wave of corporate restructuring and government downsizing that swept through the labour market in the 1980s and early 1990s. But those who still hold good jobs tend to be the older workers whose experience and seniority have allowed them to hang on to secure positions.

Some blame employers, including governments, who have frozen new hiring, whittled the size of their core staffs down to a fraction of what it was, and offer few if any career-track, entry-level jobs. Others say the problem is the school system, which is not providing youth with adequate skills for the labour market. Still others point to free trade or large impersonal forces like globalization and technological change.

Some blame bad luck. Demographer David Foot says that if you were lucky enough to be born in 1937, you were a member of a small cohort and had few competitors for good jobs as you came of age during the golden years of postwar expansion.[2] You watched the value of your house increase by many times during your prime years, and now you look forward to a comfortable retirement. If you were born during the early 1960s, however, you have struggled to compete with older members of your cohort, seen property values plummet shortly after you bought a house, and have not yet saved enough to survive a year of unemployment. Foot says the prospects for what he calls the "baby busters" — those born between 1967 and 1979 — are better because they are members of a small cohort. Although they experienced tough economic times in the early 1990s, they will eventually do better than the late members of the boomer generation because employers prefer younger workers for entry-level jobs.

Unfortunately for the baby busters, David Foot has been wrong before. In 1986 he predicted that the problem of youth unemployment would evaporate by 1994 due to the declining share of the total labour force made up of fifteen- to twenty-four-year-olds.[3] This has clearly not been the case. Foot's miscalculation arises from his contention that demography is "two-thirds of everything." It may be an advantage to be a member of a smaller cohort, all other things being equal, but other things never are equal. Demography is one factor influencing the situation of youth coming of age now, but it is only one among several, and not necessarily the most important. A long list of factors — the changing economy, new technology, global competition, employer practices, rising education costs, school curricula, weak or inappropriate skills, as well as demography and changing social attitudes to gender roles and family life — are altering the prospects of youth and their process of coming of age in Canada. This is not even to mention the differences within the generation — their gender, the class backgrounds of their families, the regions they live in, their language, ethnic, and racial groups, their varying aptitudes and abilities. To point to a single factor as a ground for optimism may be heartening, but it is misleading.

Undue pessimism is equally misleading and possibly more harmful. In the current environment, public opinion about youth's prospects is decidedly negative. A 1995 poll commissioned by *Maclean's* magazine and the CBC found "alarming levels of general pessimism" in Canada over employment prospects and the future quality of life. Many of those polled believed that the lives of the next generation would be more deprived than the lives of people then in their prime.[4] Two Angus Reid polls, one in 1989 and the other in 1995, showed a rapid decline in the optimism of youth themselves. In 1989, 65 per cent of Canadians aged eighteen to thirty-four believed that they would eventually be "better off" financially than their parents. In 1995, only 29 per cent of younger Canadians held this belief.[5]

A negative view of the future, whether valid or not, has a powerful impact on the present. People who believe that conditions in the future are going to be worse, and who have a healthy degree of self-respect and personal ambition, are much more likely to search for the individual solutions that will ensure that they and those close to them are the exceptions. They are less likely to have faith in social solutions that seek to improve conditions for everyone. But this pessimistic outlook, if widely shared, could turn out to be self-fulfilling. If there is no faith in social solutions, it is unlikely that we will ever try them out.

My point of departure in this discussion is the anxiety Canadians feel about the prospects for youth, but my own assumptions are neither optimistic nor pessimistic. Anxiety itself is a factor in the current situation, and there are good reasons for it. Let us carefully examine these reasons and consider what we can do about them. My objective is not to advise individuals on how they can thrive in these seemingly dark days, nor is it to appall readers with shocking tales of the experiences of youth. I am not seeking to find the blame in inept governments, short-sighted employers, inadequate schools, or young people themselves. My objective is to provide a guide through the terrain that youth are encountering as they come of age in the current Canadian economy and to consider how, as a society, we might act to assist their transitions to adulthood.

><

This book is essentially about the difficulties of coming of age. Youth, as I use the term here, is not a particular age range; it is a social status. The term describes a period in life in which a person is dependent or semi-dependent, usually on his or her family, for material support. This period can vary in length from one individual to another and from one generation to another, depending on social and economic conditions.

Youth is a precious time that should be enjoyed for its own sake, but ultimately all youth face one central challenge: the passage to adulthood, coming of age, achieving independence. This passage has many dimensions — economic, social, psychological, legal — which are often separated out for analysis but which in the lives of young people themselves are interconnected. Those who study the phenomenon use a number of key milestones as indicators: leaving school, leaving the family home, establishing a livelihood, setting up an independent household, marriage or cohabitation, and parenthood. Not all of these need to be realized for adult status to be achieved, but being an adult means at least having the potential to achieve them.[6]

There has never been a fixed, proper sequence in which the milestones of the passage should be achieved, nor is there any definite age level at which they should be passed. Norms vary over time and even among different groups within the same generation. Coming of age can vary with changes in the economy, especially the labour market, changing attitudes to gender roles, work, and family life, and changes to the social and economic policies of the state. My focus is on the experiences

of those who are coming of age now — the particular conditions they face and the issues raised for us as a society — but I believe that we can also gain a useful perspective by comparing these experiences to those of other generations.

Age is only one type of social status. Youth are divided into different social classes. Their parents have different types of occupations, and their families have different levels of wealth. They live in different kinds of neighbourhoods, and they may have different beliefs, perceptions, attitudes, and behaviours that arise from these family and community environments. Youth also come in two genders, and the experiences of male and female youth continue to be quite different from one another. Canadian youth also vary by ethnic background, which influences both their perceptions and their objective conditions. These three bases of social status and power — class, gender, and race or ethnicity — have been studied to a much greater extent than age or generational location for their social and economic impact on the lives of Canadians. We could add other factors to this mix, including the regions they live in, whether they live in rural areas, small towns, or large cities, and whether they are limited by disabilities. All of these factors can have a powerful impact on coming of age. A young man growing up in a poor, rural family in the Annapolis Valley of Nova Scotia, a young woman coming of age in a Haitian family in Montreal, a young member of a Cree community on the Prairies, a youth from a middle-class suburb of Victoria — each begins with different resources, receives different expectations from family, peers, authorities, and media, encounters different opportunities and risks in the world, and develops different aspirations and strategies for achieving adult status in response. General trends play themselves out in the lives of all youth but can have quite different effects on different groups.

><

Economic and social changes are destabilizing the process of coming of age in Canada and frustrating the efforts of large numbers of youth to achieve adult status. Changes in the labour market, in the capacity of the welfare state, and in gender roles and relationships have combined to create a high degree of risk and uncertainty among young people. These disruptions also affect people who are at other stages of life, of course. Large numbers of adults have had the course of their lives altered by downsizing, divorce, or the decline of welfare state entitlements. Some have been forced into early retirement or part-time work, often at drastically reduced levels of income. Youth are not the only people with problems in this society. In the midst of coming of age, however, youth are dealing with these social and economic changes all at once.

Social theorists Anthony Giddens and Ulrich Beck suggest that all social institutions and behaviour are becoming detraditionalized in this period of our history.[7] That is, social roles and commitments are no longer unquestioned traditions; they have become a matter of choice. In fact, they demand choices. Within a brief period of their lives young people are confronted with the choice of whether to pursue postsecondary education, and if so in which field of study, with a view to what kind of occupation and with what financial implications. They must decide where to live, and with whom, whether to marry, cohabit, or remain single, whether to have children or not. These and the myriad secondary choices that accompany them must be made consciously, not accepted as givens. A young man may still decide to take up the occupation of his father, if this is possible; a young woman may still decide to stay at home with her children, if she can afford it. But even these options demand active choices; they are no longer unquestioned traditions.

In other words, a much higher degree of personal freedom is now involved in coming of age, but it is constrained by the range of choices available, and there is a price to be paid for it. Gender, for example, remains a powerful conditioner of occupational choice. In principle, girls and young women can freely aspire to be firefighters, engineers, or electricians, and some do, but in practice few women choose these occupations, in large part because they have heard about the daily struggles to be accepted as an equal in a male-dominated workplace. It can be easier to choose to be a teacher, a social worker, or a secretary.[8] Social-class background also shapes a young person's perceptions of what is desirable and possible. There is much evidence to show that youth from low-income families are less likely to complete high school and more likely to be streamed into terminal programs if they do. Region, race, first language, and other factors cut across gender and class to shape both the perceptions and the actual opportunities available to youth as they come of age.

Yet there is a mythical truth to the high degree of personal freedom of choice available to this generation of youth, both male and female. All aspects of life demand choices. Nothing is to be taken for granted. It is the Horatio Alger myth updated to the present — you can choose to be whomever you want to be. The bright side of this story is found in media portrayals of young people who have fashioned careers and identities for themselves from the available materials of the postindustrial economy — entrepreneurs, filmmakers, actors, environmental activists, athletes, computer geniuses — young people who have refused to be beaten by the tough economic times.[9] This is a powerful narrative. What parents would tell their children they cannot be all they want to be?

The dark side of this personal freedom is the growing burden of individual risk, most obvious when a young person is making choices about postsecondary studies and future occupations. Whatever choice is made involves a risk to be borne by the young person making it. If young people make the wrong choice, they will be the authors of their own misfortunes. In this gamble, traditional choices are perhaps the riskiest of all. The young man who chooses to follow the occupation of his father — whether of fisherman, steelworker, teacher, civil servant, or dentist — bears at least as much risk as the one who makes a non-traditional choice, probably more. The young woman who forsakes her career ambitions to stay at home to care for her children risks the painful discovery that poverty is, as Barbara Ehrenreich puts it, "just a husband away."[10] The forms of social insurance our society has developed against such risks — the social safety net of welfare and unemployment insurance, union membership, collective agreements, and stable employment contracts — have been weakened over the past two decades, leaving individuals exposed to a wide variety of incalculable and uninsurable risks.

The price to be paid for this personal freedom, then, is self-insurance — and for the great majority of youth leaving behind the support of their families this protection can only be found in the labour market. The one, central task in coming of age for almost all members of our society is to establish an independent livelihood. Most adult Canadians rely upon the labour market completely for their livelihoods, at least until they are approaching retirement age in their fifties and sixties. But access to the labour market is governed by access to the education system. These two institutions loom over the lives of young people with almost the same totality that the manor and the church once did in feudal society. To be denied a place in either is to be cast into the outer darkness or, as we say nowadays, to become socially marginalized.

2 Coming of Age in Canada: 1850-1945

We often assume that there is a normal, natural process of coming of age that involves growing up in the family home, attending school until one leaves it for good, finding a job, establishing an independent household, and then, for most, marrying and having children. But coming of age has rarely, if ever, been this kind of linear, orderly process. For most generations since the beginning of the industrial period, it has been liable to pitfalls, setbacks, and reversals.[1] If coming of age means making one's way from youthful dependence to adult independence, the passage takes young people through a landscape of risks and opportunities created by the institutions, practices, beliefs, and specific historical circumstances of the day.

Canada's past century and a half have witnessed five distinct periods of social and economic history. Each period shaped the life experiences of young people and framed the challenge of coming of age. Until the middle of the nineteenth century, Canada was a preindustrial society. Most people gained a living through agricultural production on family farms, while in the towns independent commercial and artisanal enterprises dominated the economy. From the 1840s to the 1890s, Canada experienced its first industrial revolution. Wage labour gradually surpassed the independent production of farms and workshops as a means of survival for most people. Around the turn of the century came the beginnings of a second industrial revolution, marked by the growth of large corporations, new labour-saving technology, and new forms of organizing production. This period ended in the catastrophes of the Great Depression and the Second World War. The postwar period, from 1945 to the mid-1970s, sometimes called "the golden age," saw the construction of a welfare state, rapid economic growth, strong unionization in the dominant sectors of the economy, and qualitative improvements in the standard of living of most Canadians. The fifth period, which continues today, is sometimes called the postindustrial economy, the service economy, or simply "the new economy."

There were no well-defined moments of transition between these periods. Elements of earlier times continued to exist well into later periods. For example, family farms and artisanal production persisted throughout the nineteenth and twentieth centuries, although other forms of economic and social organization surpassed them.[2]

Throughout these periods of our history, four institutions have played especially important roles in the lives of youth and the transition to adult independence: the family, education system, labour market, and state.[3] As the broad social and economic changes of each period have taken hold, changes in these major institutions have created shifting configurations of risk and opportunity for youth.

Preindustrial Canada

In the mid-nineteenth century most people in the British North American colonies still lived on family farms, and the lives of children and youth were governed by the demands and rhythms of rural life. Children were assigned chores at an early age — feeding animals, tending vegetable gardens — and gradually took on heavier tasks and more demanding responsibilities as they grew older. Boys were responsible for driving horses, ploughing, and construction work. Girls learned how to make clothes, prepare meals, and process food. School attendance was sporadic and irregular in the rural areas; public school systems did not exist before the late 1840s. Still, many parents formed local groups to hire teachers to provide their children with a basic education, and literacy rates were comparatively high. To encourage bible study many Protestant churches trained their congregations in literacy skills. In general, the knowledge, skills, and attitudes needed for rural life were learned in the family and the church.[4]

Rural youth, especially boys, would frequently leave home to work elsewhere — in lumber camps, on log drives, fishing boats, and road construction crews, or in jobs in town. Coming of age began with responsible work in the household, often passed through a phase of earning independent income off-farm during the teens and twenties, and culminated with establishing an independent household and marriage. The children who were not heirs to the family farm usually left the family home when they got married. They might pioneer an independent homestead elsewhere or take over a portion of the family estate. In either case a new home was a major investment, and it usually took several years of work to earn cash savings, delaying marriage well past the age of sexual maturity.

Most people then viewed marriage as a lifetime commitment and a necessary prerequisite to living together as a couple and having children. About 90 per cent of men and women born in the first half of the nineteenth century eventually married. Among those born between 1821 and 1830, for example, the average age at first marriage was twenty-six for men and twenty-three for women. The average age at marriage and the percentage who never married both increased as the changes later in the century destabilized social and economic life.[5]

Coming of age in the preindustrial towns of British North America was similar to rural life in several ways, despite differences in the occupational structure. Social historian Michael Katz provides a description of growing up in Hamilton, Ontario (then Canada West), in the mid-nineteenth century as Hamilton became an industrial city.[6] In 1851 Hamilton, with a population of fourteen thousand, was a port and commercial centre serving the agricultural economy of the surrounding area. In its social structure and distribution of occupations, it was similar to other preindustrial cities in Canada and the United States at the time. At the top, representing no more than a tenth of the population, was a male elite of businessmen and professionals in whom economic, social, and political power overlapped. In the middle were men in a variety of skilled trades — bakers, tinsmiths, tailors, shoemakers, carpenters, builders — as well as less prosperous commercial occupations. At the bottom were unskilled labourers, who made up about a quarter of the male population. Very few married women had occupations outside the home, but prior to marriage many young women worked as domestic servants, dressmakers, seamstresses, or milliners.

Like other communities of the era, Hamilton had sharp inequalities. The top 10 per cent of the population owned 60 per cent of the wealth in property and income, while the poorest 40 per cent owned 6 per cent. Ethnicity and religion ran parallel with the class structure. Irish

Catholics, recently arrived as refugees from the potato famine, made up a large portion of the poor, unskilled labourers; Scottish Presbyterians dominated the building trades and commercial occupations; Canadian-born Protestants predominated in banking, medicine, and law. The city also had a population of people of African ancestry, descendants of slaves who came to Canada with Loyalist slave-owners or who had escaped to Canada later on the "underground railway." Slavery had been abolished in the British Empire in 1833, and by 1851 some people of African origin in Hamilton were working in skilled trades or as small shopkeepers, while others worked as labourers.

Children grew up in their parents' homes, and from the ages of five to sixteen many of them went to school. The peak years for schooling were ages nine to eleven, the only time when over half of those in the age group were attending school. More boys than girls attended at each age level. Attendance dropped off rapidly after age eleven, and by age sixteen less than a tenth of the youth in that age group were in school. Children of the well-to-do were far more likely to attend school than those of the poor. The wealthy also kept their children in school longer. Ethnicity and religion played a part too. Irish Catholics sent less than a third of their children to school, while Scottish Presbyterians sent over 60 per cent. Larger families were also more likely to send their children to school, regardless of class, which led Katz to conclude that even at that time schools performed a babysitting function.

After the school years the experiences of young men and women diverged sharply. By age fifteen, many more young males were employed than in school. Most lived at home through the age of sixteen, but by age twenty only a quarter of them were living at home, and by age twenty-five only 14 per cent. It seems that the majority of young men left their parents' home when they found work.

♦ Large numbers of boys and young men, however, neither worked nor went to school. Katz calculates that in 1851 nearly half of the eleven- to fifteen-year-olds and about a quarter of the sixteen- to twenty-year-olds lived in a state of "partial idleness." Social reformers of the time complained that large numbers of youth roamed around the town with little or nothing to do. In nearby Toronto the Honourable John Elmsley of the Board of School Trustees deplored "the idleness and dissipation of a large number of children, who now loiter about the public streets or frequent the haunts of vice, creating the most painful emotions in every well regulated mind, and in some degree involving the imputation that the social condition of the body corporate of which they form a part cannot be of the highest order."[7]

Young, single, working men who did not live with their parents boarded in another household; it was virtually unknown for single people to live on their own. More than a quarter of households included boarders. Many of the boarders in Hamilton may have been young immigrants or the sons of farm families, but Katz found evidence that the sons of Hamilton families were also more likely to leave their parents' homes when they found work. He concludes that this period in a young man's life was one of "semi-autonomy," a period in which a young man was earning an income of his own and living outside his parents' direct supervision, but still subject to the social control of the host family and not yet able to establish an independent household of his own.

Some of these young men were apprentices living in the homes of their masters while they learned a trade. The master, mobilizing the labour of his wife and daughters, typically provided his apprentices with food, clothing, and bedding as part of the contract. A young man could usually achieve journeyman status after five years of apprenticeship, two years less than in England.

Most men in Hamilton at that time married late in their twenties, usually not before the age of twenty-five. In 1851, two out of five men were still unmarried at the age of thirty. This was not due to a lack of women of marriageable age. In most cases it seems likely to have been for economic reasons. As in the rural areas, men were expected to have the resources to set up an independent household before they married. Couples very rarely lived in their parents' home after marriage. The late marriage age therefore reflects the difficulties encountered by young men in earning sufficient income and savings to establish an independent household.

Young women left home at about the same age as young men, if not earlier. A third of them were working as domestic servants and living with their employers by age thirteen. The number increased to 40 per cent by age seventeen. A further 10 per cent of young women lived as boarders while they were employed elsewhere, usually as seamstresses, dressmakers, or milliners. The percentage of young women who worked in the Hamilton labour force peaked at just over 50 per cent at the age of nineteen and declined thereafter as they married. Women tended to marry in their early twenties, several years younger than men, and most left the paid workforce at that point.

More young women than men experienced a time when they neither attended school nor had a job, during which time they lived at home and continued to be dependent on their parents. All but the wealthiest no doubt contributed to the domestic work of the household.

This may be seen as a period of preparation for marriage, but it also reflects the limited scope for women in the urban labour force before the industrial period. Most young women looked forward to married life as their career, which may account in large part for their earlier marriages. Almost no married women in the census of 1851 listed any occupation. Of those aged thirty, 83 per cent were married and only 15 per cent were employed.

But as Katz shows, in the decades following 1851 the picture began to change. As economic and social conditions altered, the experience of young people as they encountered the key milestones — leaving school, finding employment, leaving home, marriage, establishing an independent household — changed. A depression in 1857 ended a period of economic growth and diminished job opportunities. By 1861 a recovery was underway, but youth seemed to be the last to benefit. In 1851 a significant number of young men had worked in the trades practised by their fathers; a decade later a much smaller proportion did so. Youth participation in crafts that were in decline dropped disproportionately to that of older age groups, particularly in the clothing trades, which had been transformed by the introduction of the sewing machine during the 1850s. For example, the percentage of the city's tailors who were under the age of thirty dropped from 40 per cent to 19 per cent between 1851 and 1861.

The combined effect of increased schooling and lack of employment opportunities resulted in a much larger proportion of young men and women living at home with their parents in 1861 than in 1851. The majority of young men now lived at home until the age of twenty-one. Those away from home still lived as boarders, but the incidence of boarding declined steeply. The middle classes, still recovering from the depression, also hired fewer servants, reducing the job opportunities for young women.

Both sexes, therefore, experienced an increased period of dependency. This might have seemed at the time to be a short-term phenomenon, due to the economic downturn, but it continued to increase in the years that followed. Young men married even later after the depression, but the length of the period of semi-autonomy contracted due to the extended period of dependency on their parents. Young women also stayed at home longer, but not to the same degree as men, perhaps because the employment prospects for domestic servants were not as severely harmed. However, migration of young men in search of work, and the delayed age of marriage of those who remained, meant that young women's prospects for marriage declined.

Katz, then, found significant changes in the process of coming of age in just one decade. Between 1851 and 1861 school attendance increased significantly due to the institution of public schooling. The period in which young people remained at home, dependent on their parents, was extended. There was a large increase in unemployment among the sixteen- to twenty-year-olds, and a reduced participation of young men in declining crafts. The age of marriage was delayed further, but the period of semi-autonomy was reduced because of the longer period spent at home. Finally, a migration of young men reduced the prospects for marriage of the young women, and, depending on their destinations, probably for the young men as well. Just as it would be almost a century and a half later, it would have been difficult in 1861 to say which of these changes were short-term and cyclical, and which represented a long-term, structural shift in the social and economic life of youth.

The Early Industrial Period

Beginning in the 1840s, the economies of the British North American colonies began to industrialize. Factories and other workplaces owned by industrial capitalists employing wage labour emerged as the new growth centres of the economy. Many traditional crafts went into decline, as did the percentage of the population living on farms. After the depression of the late 1850s this trend accelerated through the 1860s and into the 1870s as the industrial economy expanded rapidly.

In the growing urban centres, a family's social class shaped the fortunes of its youth. Social historian Bettina Bradbury found that in Montreal unskilled labourers, constrained by low wages, tended to marry later than members of other classes, have fewer children, and, once their children were old enough to earn wages, keep them at home for shorter periods. Their children entered the labour market at an early age to supplement the meagre wages of their fathers, but had fewer incentives to remain in the family home for long. The same was true for the children of skilled craftsmen in the "injured trades" — the trades such as tailoring and shoemaking that were losing out to factory production.[8] Children of the more secure skilled workers as well as middle-class businessmen and professionals, meanwhile, were more likely to stay at home and better able to continue their schooling.

Bradbury's detailed calculations show that the wages paid to labourers in Montreal during this period were inadequate to meet the basic needs of a family for food and shelter, let alone clothing, footwear, school fees, and other necessities. This resulted in a high incidence of poverty when they married and had young children at home. But as the children became old enough to work they were able to supplement the family income. The family entered the most prosperous stage of its life cycle when two, three, or more of its children were working and contributing their wages to the household's revenue. As the offspring moved away, however, the parents tended to sink again into poverty and had dismal prospects for their old age.[9]

The employment of children and youth was important not only to the survival strategies of their families but also to the business strategies of early industrial capitalists. Before the 1880s no province had any legislation governing the employment of children, and there was no agreement on the appropriate age at which youth should begin to work full-time for wages. In some cases children entered full-time wage labour before the age of ten, but this was unusual. Even poor parents preferred to send their children to school until age eleven or twelve if they could manage to do so. After that age, however, the sons and daughters of working-class families went out to work in the sawmills, coal mines, canning factories, cotton mills, and other workplaces of the early industrial period. A few were still able to enter preindustrial apprenticeships and learn skilled trades, particularly in occupations that had not yet been undermined by industrialization — such as printing, blacksmithing, and baking for boys, and dressmaking and millinery for girls — but these opportunities became increasingly rare. More frequently boys were assigned to helping roles — fetching, carrying, sweeping — or to low-skill production jobs that had been redesigned, and in some cases mechanized, so that they could be performed by low-wage child labour. Girls entered the labour market less frequently than boys and usually at a slightly older age, and they did not have the same jobs as their brothers. Domestic service was still a common role for girls, but in the industrializing economy they also found work in canning, cigar rolling, packing end products, and other simple manual tasks in factories.

Some employers called these young workers "apprentices," but this was a debasement of the term. They were not learning to be skilled artisans. On the contrary, they were frequently deployed strategically into redesigned work tasks that narrowed the roles of adult craftsmen, allowing employers to eliminate skilled positions and reduce labour costs — a foreshadowing of the redesigned labour processes that were to appear in the early twentieth century. Children and youth did not advance from these jobs into journeyman status but only to heavier and somewhat better-paid adult work. As labour historian Craig Heron observes, they were treated like adult workers in every way but in their wages. "To take a stark example," he writes, "twelve-year-old boys worked in Ottawa lumber mills six days a week from 6 a.m. to 6:30 p.m., with fifty minutes at noon for lunch and frequent overtime, for forty cents or less a day." Not surprisingly, employers found them "very saving and economical."[10]

Child labour became the target of the Victorian reform movement in Canada as in other industrializing countries, and by the 1880s factory acts in several provinces defined the legal age limit for wage labour. In Ontario, for example, the age requirement was set at twelve for boys and fourteen for girls in 1886, then raised to fourteen for both sexes in 1895.

In 1891 the Ontario government also introduced compulsory schooling for all children to the age of fourteen, attacking the problem from another direction. This represented the latest advance in half a century of efforts to promote public school systems in the Canadian provinces. The school promoters — led by reformers such as Egerton Ryerson in Ontario and Alexander Forrester in Nova Scotia — were part of an energetic new middle class that believed in social progress, Christian virtues, and the transformation of a diverse and unpredictable mass of people, including large numbers of new immigrants, into respectable citizens prepared to take their proper places in the social order. Influenced by similar movements in the United States and Europe, these men aimed to create a free, universal, centralized, graded, and compulsory system of education for all classes, especially the poorest. The schools would produce graduates who were not only trained in basic skills but also prepared for employment befitting their social class. The graduates would also be morally sound and patriotic. "By Education," Ryerson wrote in his *Report on a System of Public Elementary Instruction* in 1846, "I mean not the mere acquisition of certain arts, or of certain branches of knowledge, but that instruction and discipline which qualify and dispose the subjects of it for their appropriate duties and employment of life, as Christians, as persons of business and also as members of the civil community in which they live."[11]

Historians debate the motives of the school reformers. The traditional view is that they were enlightened benefactors, foes of the reactionary ruling elites, seeking to create school systems that would give all citizens the basic skills and moral foundation required to function in society.[12] Historians in the 1970s revised this image, portraying the reformers as concerned primarily with establishing a system of social control in a rapidly urbanizing society with all of its attendant evils —

crime, poverty, drunkenness, and juvenile delinquency. The purpose of schools, by this account, was essentially conservative; it was to socialize and channel youth into appropriate roles in society on the basis of their class, gender, and race.[13] Another interpretation stresses the importance to the reformers of schooling as the basis of a common citizenship. Free, universal education was to be a public good that would create a citizenry from out of the chaos of political strife and waves of immigration, thereby laying the foundation in civil society for the Canadian state and the system of liberal democracy that developed in the second half of the century.[14]

No doubt the minds of Victorian reformers could embrace all of these motives. There is evidence for each of these interpretations in their speeches and writings. In any case, as historian Paul Axelrod points out, the spread of public schooling was far from being just a top-down project. Free, universal public education financed from local taxes and provincial subsidies received an enthusiastic popular response. Between 1841 and 1871 the number of students in publicly controlled day schools in Canada rose fivefold, from 160,000 to 800,000, and by 1901 some 1.1 million students were enrolled in public schools. Although all jurisdictions eventually made schooling compulsory, that move tended to follow, not precede, large-scale participation.[15]

Many youth, to be sure, followed a pattern of irregular attendance. Axelrod estimates that by 1900, only six out of ten Canadian youth aged five to fifteen attended school regularly. Rural attendance rates lagged behind those in urban areas, because the labour of farm youth continued to be in demand at home, especially in spring and fall. Girls were less likely to have jobs than boys and therefore more likely to be in school, but working-class youth of both sexes were more likely to have irregular attendance and to leave the school system earlier than middle-class youth. This was not only due to labour-market participation. For the poorest families, the cost of books, supplies, and even proper shoes and clothing was also a barrier to attendance. In short, this transformation in the life experience of youth happened unevenly by region and social class, but in general the pattern was one of acceptance and support for this new institution, the public school. "Ordinary Canadians," Axelrod says, "did not really need to be dragged to the schoolhouse door, though the poorest among them found it difficult to attend regularly. They too hoped to reap the benefits of society's investment in public schools."[16]

Still, those who maintain that public schools were intended as a new system of social control have considerable evidence on their side. Rote learning was a common teaching method, and the curriculum stressed not only reading and writing but also "respectable" grammar and enunciation, patriotism, and the virtues of honesty, obedience, and punctuality. Teachers enforced this regime with corporal punishment when necessary. Kindly or not, the intention was clearly to shape the attitudes and behaviour of young people to fit the expectations of the dominant culture. This is most evident in the way compulsory schooling was imposed on many aboriginal children and youth. Using its authority under the British North America Act of 1867 and the Indian Act of 1876 and 1880, the federal government in partnership with Christian missionaries established residential schools for aboriginal youth away from their home communities. The purpose was frankly assimilationist. Students were required to adopt European dress and hair styles, to speak English, and to follow a curriculum of basic education and manual training designed to prepare them to function in the bottom layers of the Canadian economy and society. The coercive atmosphere of the schools lent itself easily to widespread incidents of physical and sexual abuse by school authorities, many of which have only come to light in recent years. The anger of aboriginal youth and their parents at this systematic mistreatment fuelled resistance to the residential schools. Many students ran away and refused to return. Schools within aboriginal communities might have respected the indigenous culture and identity, but the federal government provided inadequate resources to meet that end. As a result, as recently as the middle of the twentieth century two-fifths of aboriginal people in Canada over the age of five had no formal schooling at all.[17]

Educational historian Alison Prentice argues that it was the conscious objective of Ontario's school reformers to reduce the public role and influence of the churches in the education of youth and to replace them with state institutions that would cultivate common civic virtues and non-sectarian Christian values in all citizens. They also urged a more limited view of the family in the socialization of youth. Both church and family were to restrict themselves to the sphere of private life, while the state through its schools took responsibility for the formal training of youth in the skills and virtues required for their public roles as citizens and workers.[18]

Of course, the reformers did not succeed entirely in this mission. Denominational schools continued to play a major role in the education of youth in Newfoundland, Quebec, and Ontario, and their role was even enshrined in the British North America Act. But state-run public schools had staked a claim on the lives of youth, and over the next century their role was to expand enormously while the role and influence of churches and the family receded.

Public secondary schools were established throughout English-speaking Canada in the second half of the nineteenth century. Attended primarily by the sons and daughters of the middle classes, they concentrated on the academic subjects — English, history, modern languages, science, the classics, and mathematics. This subject-matter served to refine their "mental culture" and prepare those who continued for entry to professional training or universities. By 1900, only one in ten fifteen-to nineteen-year-olds attended secondary school, boys and girls in equal numbers. In Quebec, after their primary schooling francophone males destined for university and the professions attended classical colleges, where they encountered a rigorous curriculum equivalent to a Bachelor of Arts university program.[19]

Children of the well-to-do had always had access to private schooling, and despite the establishment of public primary and secondary school systems throughout Canada their parents continued to send them to elite "independent" schools, such as Upper Canada College in Toronto, Halifax Ladies' School, and University School in Victoria, B.C. In these places they underwent a regime of classical education and character development designed to prepare them for political, social, and economic leadership. There, too, they began to establish the networks with others of their generation and class that would sustain their social position throughout their adult careers.

The Second Industrial Revolution

The factories of Canada's first industrial revolution tended to be small, rarely employing more than two hundred workers. Most were locally owned and controlled, dispersed across the Maritimes, Quebec, and Ontario, producing goods largely for local markets. The technology was not yet complex, and skilled craftsmen still played a critical role in production even if they were no longer independent artisans.

During the second industrial revolution, which began in the 1890s and picked up momentum in the early twentieth century, large corporations came to dominate the landscape, transforming the leading Canadian industries into oligopolies controlled by a small business elite. U.S. corporations began to arrive and set up operations inside Canada's tariff wall, bringing with them new technology and methods of organizing production. Many new industries came into existence, including steel, pulp and paper, chemicals, electrical, automobiles, and hardrock mining. They employed large-scale production methods and consolidated much of their production in large centres, especially in Ontario and Quebec.

S.S.F.C.
RESOURCES
CENTRE

The Maritimes entered a long period of deindustrialization and economic decline. Meanwhile, fuelled by world demand, the resource-based economies of Western Canada grew quickly and provided markets for the manufactured goods of Central Canada.

The United States was about twenty years ahead of Canada in this economic transformation and had developed new methods to accomplish the perennial imperatives of the market economy — reducing costs and maximizing profits. U.S. business brought two interrelated sets of tools to these tasks: new labour-saving technology and new ways of organizing production. Management introduced new machinery that sharply reduced the need for many of the skilled craftsmen who had dominated the industries of the nineteenth century. At the same time, companies organized production increasingly along the principles of "scientific management," a set of methods developed by U.S. engineer Frederick Taylor and which as a result became known as "Taylorism." Management succeeded in reducing the need for skilled craftsmen even further as they assigned semi-skilled workers precise, repetitive manual tasks in the operation of the new machinery. Craft workers declined to a minority of the industrial labour force, their unions and their self-confidence effectively undermined by the 1920s.[20]

Mechanization of agriculture also reduced the need for labour in rural areas. The percentage of the workforce engaged in agriculture declined from half of all workers in 1867 to two-fifths in 1901 and a third by 1921.[21] The shift away from farm life and into towns and cities was especially strong among youth. The category "farmer's son" in the Canadian census went from 17 per cent of the male workforce in 1891 to just 4 per cent in 1911.[22] The child labour laws, compulsory schooling, new production methods, and large waves of immigration changed the prospects for youth in the labour market. Children under fifteen were now almost completely shut out. Employment opportunities for young men continued to decline in the skilled craft occupations, but semi-skilled jobs opened up in factories, trade, and transportation. Young men also continued to migrate to remote areas to make money in Canada's resource extraction industries, especially logging and mining.

Young women entered the paid workforce in greater numbers than ever before, but their access to the labour market was limited in several ways. In her study of women in the Canadian clothing industry from 1890 to 1940, Mercedes Steedman observes that when they entered the labour market women were given the sorts of jobs that women were expected to do. The ten leading occupations of women in 1891 were domestic servant, dressmaker, seamstress, tailoress, saleswoman, teacher, farmer, housekeeper, laundress, and milliner, in that order. As this list suggests, female workers tended to be relegated to job ghettoes — personal services, parts of the clothing industry, and elementary school teaching — in which they received rates of pay that were considerably less than the wages paid to men doing similar or identical work.[23] By 1911 new female occupations were beginning to appear — office workers, nurses, and telephone operators, for example — but the same principles applied. These jobs were defined as female work and came with wage rates much lower than men's.

Steedman identifies two related ideologies that allowed this situation to be perceived as natural and just. The Victorian idealization of femininity reinforced the view that a woman's proper adult role was to be a wife and mother, managing her home and raising her children. Participation in the labour market was to be a brief episode in a young woman's life between the time she left school and the time she married. As in preindustrial Hamilton, most women workers were young and single. Almost half the female labour force in 1911 was under twenty-five. The low wages were deemed appropriate because the income was supplementary to the earnings of the women's fathers. If a woman did continue to work after marriage — and as late as 1921 over four-fifths of employed women were single — her wages were viewed as supplementary to those of her husband. A married woman's unpaid economic role was to prepare food and clothing for her family, to care for her children, to manage her household frugally, and often to earn a little income on the side by taking in boarders. The system ensured that young women would remain dependent on their families, that married women would be dependent on their husbands, and that many older unmarried women and single mothers would live in poverty.

Complementing the idealization of femininity was the ideology of the family wage. From the earliest days of trade union organizing one of the labour movement's main demands was for wage levels high enough to allow a man to support his wife and children. As Steedman points out, in the clothing industry these two ideologies together led working men to become accomplices in the reduction of women's wages. The system undermined men's wage levels too, because women's lower wages caused a downward pressure on the men's.

Not all women accepted the ideologies that kept them confined to low-wage job ghettoes and unpaid work in the home. Cultural values varied among the different ethnic groups. Working-class Jewish women with roots in Eastern Europe, for example, were not at all reluctant to work outside the home or to engage in trade union organizing, both before and after marriage. During a general strike of garment industry workers in Montreal in 1910, women were reported to be asking, "Why should men demand and receive more than twice as much pay as we get, when our cost of living is equally high and we have the same skills in the trade?"[24]

》∞〈

During the first three decades of the twentieth century, concerns about prospects for youth in the changing industrial economy gave rise to another round of educational reform. Educators and government authorities were especially worried about boys who dropped out as soon as they reached the age of fourteen, fearing that they faced dim prospects in low-wage jobs or unemployment. Recalling Ryerson and the Victorian school promoters, they expressed anxiety over the growing body of unemployed, idle youth. As they would do repeatedly throughout the twentieth century, reformers defined the problem not as dwindling job opportunities for youth but as the failure of youth to prepare themselves adequately for a changing labour market. More schooling, they believed, was necessary to head off growing rates of youth crime, poverty, and vagrancy. "No State is safe if only some of its social units are educated," Ontario's Minister of Education declared in 1919 as he introduced legislation to extend compulsory schooling to age sixteen.[25]

Vocationalism — advocacy of changes to the school curriculum to provide youth of both sexes with training that would be more relevant to their future occupations — was the leading thrust of this reform movement. Critical of elementary and secondary education for being too academic and serving only the small percentage of students who went on to further studies, reformers called for new curricula in the fields of technical and industrial skills, commercial and business education, and domestic science and home economics.

Demands both from educational reformers and industrial employers led the federal government to create a Royal Commission on Industrial Training and Technical Education in 1909.[26] The Commission travelled across Canada and to the United States and Europe, finally reporting in 1913. The commissioners noted with alarm the rapid growth of the urban population. Between 1901 and 1911, while Canada's population as a whole grew by 34 per cent, the urban population in particular grew by 62 per cent. Immigration, the mechanization of agriculture, the greater availability of jobs, schools, and other services in urban areas — and what the Commission called "the attractiveness to young people of the amusements and excitements afforded by town and city life" —

combined to make Canadian society increasingly urban.[27] Vocational education was proposed as a way to help these youth perform more capably and adapt to this new economy. Advocates pointed to the withering of the apprenticeship system with the decline of craft occupations and called for the introduction of programs of study, especially in secondary schools, that would be relevant to the occupational expectations of the majority of students, not just those who expected to continue on to university and professional careers.

The suggestion that critical social issues should be addressed by changes to the education system has since become a time-honoured tradition in Canada. The debates over vocationalism anticipated the controversy over educational reform in the 1990s. Advocates of vocational education argued that Canada was falling behind other countries in its capacity to educate its youth "to become the best artisans, farmers and housekeepers in the world." Educational work was becoming "bookish in the extreme," and schools had "few points of contact with or relation to industrial, agricultural, or housekeeping life."[28] The commissioners maintained that this situation was unfair to those who expected to be working in factories, workshops, farms, and fishing boats or performing the domestic role of women in the home. These students, they said, saw little in their studies that would help them later on and tended to drop out of school at the first opportunity.

The Canadian Manufacturers' Association, speaking for industrial employers, complained to the Royal Commission that Canada was suffering from a shortage of "competent, well-trained mechanical experts to act as foremen, superintendents, managers, etc." The only way many employers could get the skilled workers they needed was to recruit them from Europe and the United States or, as a last resort, to train them themselves. To correct this situation, the CMA called upon the federal government to establish a national technical education system at the secondary level to turn out suitably qualified workers for Canadian industries.[29]

The opponents of vocational education argued that the practice would lead to overspecialization and further divide the population between those going on to the professions and those entering manual occupations. They believed that a common curriculum for all students was still the best preparation for life, regardless of social class.[30] Today many historians agree with this analysis. They see the reformers as concerned primarily with the efficient streaming and slotting of students, training youth to fit smoothly and obediently into the new set of social and technical relations emerging in workplaces, as well as reinforcing traditional gender roles and status.[31]

A different view is that the field of vocational education was a contested terrain, just as the education system still is today. It did not need to be a system for delivering a trained and compliant workforce to employers at public expense. With appropriate subject-matter and teaching methods, vocational training could equally serve to liberate youth from old gender roles and class categories, prepare them to question workplace roles and structures, and develop both intellectual and manual skills that would improve their lives and livelihoods. At its best, it could break down the barriers between academic and manual work, between theory and practice, and serve, up to a point, as a new common curriculum for all students.[32] A close reading of the Royal Commission's report suggests that the commissioners were guided to some extent by a broad, humanistic purpose. "It must be kept in mind," they wrote, "that the chief object of industrial training and technical education must be the personal welfare of the individuals who are to participate in it; second, the prosperity and strength of the State; and third, the advancement and improvement of industry as such, and that only as consistent with and subordinate to the other two. . . . The attempt must be made to meet the needs of all the people, with care that none shall be debased by the occupations for which they are prepared, and none shall be debarred from earning satisfaction, as well as satisfactory wages, from labour."[33]

Vocational education in secondary schools never did develop in this way. It spread slowly during the years between the two world wars and contributed to increased school attendance by working-class youth, but it was avoided by middle- and upper-class youth and their parents.[34] There is little doubt that it served as a way of channelling working-class youth into lower-status jobs. Educators themselves reinforced the primacy of academic learning over vocational content.[35] Some working-class youth learned skills that made a positive difference in their lives. Jane Gaskell observes that young women in particular benefited from commercial education that gave them occupational alternatives that had not been available before.[36] Canadian manufacturers, however, continued to rely on immigration from Europe for their supply of skilled workers. The adoption in industry of the methods of scientific management led to a three-tier system of technical skills in the leading industries. University-trained engineers designed and managed production; skilled workers served as foremen and superintendents; and the majority of workers carried out routine tasks that did not require extensive technical training. Most young men in blue-collar jobs learned their skills by the "pick-up method" — that is, they were trained informally on the job

by their fellow workers, with minimal formal training provided by their employers.

Craig Heron found that working-class youth in Hamilton of the 1920s continued to drop out of school as soon as they reached the legal age of sixteen, especially if demand for their labour was strong. They found that a diploma made little difference to their prospects during good times. Many of their families still relied on the supplementary income that their children could bring in and found the extension of compulsory schooling a hardship. Apart from brief periods in the 1920s, however, demand for young workers ranged from poor to abysmal throughout the interwar years. The combination of increased years of compulsory schooling and dwindling job opportunities for youth was a new situation to which working-class families had to adapt. To compensate for the lost income, Heron found, Hamilton's working-class families became smaller during these years, with more women in them working for wages beyond the normal marriage age.[37] In Canada as a whole the average marriage age remained high, around twenty-eight for men and twenty-five for women.[38]

By 1931, 96 per cent of Canadian children nine to twelve years old were attending school regularly, with attendance rates steadily declining thereafter, from 93 per cent for thirteen-year-olds to 67 per cent for fifteen-year-olds. A distinctive youth labour market began to take shape on the margins of the economy, composed primarily of after-school and summer jobs as messengers, newspaper vendors, domestic workers, and the like. The extended period of dependence became a fixed portion of the life course, a time that came to be viewed as a normal stage of life. At the turn of the century, U.S. psychologist G. Stanley Hall had labelled it "adolescence" — a term adapted from the Latin verb *adolescere*, meaning "to become an adult." Coming of age was no longer seen as a specific occasion or moment in life but as an extended period of physical, social, and psychological maturation.

In Canada the damage caused by the worldwide Depression of the 1930s was severe. By official estimates between 1929 and 1933 at least 30 per cent of the labour force was unemployed and 20 per cent of all Canadians depended on government relief. In reality the situation was much worse, with an impact distributed unevenly across regions, social classes, and age groups. In Saskatchewan, for example, crop failure and a collapse of world wheat prices resulted in a drop in provincial income of 90 per cent in two years, forcing two-thirds of the rural population onto relief. In Ontario and Quebec, the more diversified economies and the market for manufactured goods captured behind Canada's tariff wall meant lower unemployment rates. Wages fell, but prices fell even faster, so those who had jobs or earned income from property were sometimes better off. Hardest hit were farmers, small business owners, the unemployed, and particularly the young, who had little or no access to the shrinking labour market.[39]

Before 1935 the only solution offered to massive youth unemployment was a system of relief camps for single men established in 1932 by the Conservative government of R.B. Bennett. The camps offered a bunkhouse, meals, and twenty cents a day for work clearing bush, building roads, planting trees, and constructing public buildings. Many young men went to these camps as a last resort, but anger at the low pay and bad conditions in the camps and the inadequacy of Bennett's response to the unemployment crisis sparked a strike by camp workers in British Columbia that led to the famous On to Ottawa Trek of 1935.[40] No response at all was proposed for unemployed young women at first. Young women living at home with their parents, or in any other person's home, were considered to be engaged in domestic work and were not counted as unemployed.[41]

The business, political, and religious elites of the day were acutely conscious of the difficult situation of youth. The inadequacy of the relief camps was apparent by 1935. A report prepared for the Anglican bishops of Canada, for example, concluded that the young were being demoralized, losing self-respect, and engaging in "unnatural vices" in the camps.[42] Adults worried that the lack of jobs was a disincentive to youth to stay in school, because their diplomas would not make any difference to their prospects. They also feared that the forced delay of marriage for financial reasons was leading to an increase in premarital sex. They argued that increased crime rates were the result of unemployment and saw the dire economic conditions as an explanation for the success of subversive doctrines. Mr H.A. Weir, a Nova Scotia school inspector, warned: "The rapidity with which existing political institutions may be overthrown has been amply demonstrated in those countries where unemployment, with all its attendant disillusionment and suffering, was most widespread. Youth — particularly idle youth — is quick to adopt the catch-phrase of the political propagandist."[43] The Communist Party of Canada in particular, although rigidly repressed, was active in organizing unemployed youth in the camps and elsewhere through affiliates like the Relief Camp Workers Union and the National Unemployed Workers Association.[44]

Elected to power in 1935, Mackenzie King's Liberal government had a different plan. It was King who, as a young minister of labour, had launched the Royal Commission on Industrial Training and Technical Education in 1909. Over a quarter-century later King again turned to education and training as the solution to youth problems. His government closed the relief camps and established the Dominion-Provincial Youth Training Programme, the first joint effort of the federal and provincial governments to address the problem of youth unemployment in Canada through training schemes. King expressed confidence that training would prepare youth for new jobs in the future, once the economy recovered. As Rebecca Prieger Coulter observes in her study of the

D-PYTP, the country had virtual unanimity on this point. Despite the obvious shortage of jobs, everyone from the Saskatchewan School Trustees Association and the Trades and Labour Congress to the Central Committee of the Communist Party of Canada agreed that at least part of the reason so many young people were unemployed was their lack of training for skilled or semi-skilled work. She adds that this perception of youth unemployment changed very little in the following sixty years. "The D-PYTP," Coulter writes, "established the model and rationale for a social and educational policy on youth unemployment which persists to this day."[45]

This model, which Coulter calls "warehousing," was designed primarily to keep youth off the streets and out of trouble. The training offered was substandard, often involved much more physical labour than instruction, and in some cases strongly resembled the relief camps. Certificates "of proficiency" or "of competence" at the end of the training courses were explicitly forbidden. Many of the specific projects focused heavily on "attitude adjustment" — training young people in proper behaviour and dress to please prospective employers. Despite the efforts of placement officers employed by the program, those who went through training courses showed a low success rate in finding employment. The records indicate that only 22 per cent of those enrolled in courses in 1937-38 found work, and 30 per cent in 1938-39, and even these levels were achieved by counting any job at all, no matter how brief. The main benefit, according to Coulter, was the opportunity it gave young people to escape from their isolation, especially in rural areas, and to socialize with others in the same circumstances. A lot of young people had fun on their courses while they lasted. They could offer one another mutual support and some relief from the drudgery of poverty and unemployment.

All of this ended with the war. By 1940 the D-PYTP had been transformed into the Wartime Emergency Training Programme, focused on training young workers in skills that were in demand in industry and the military. Unemployment had disappeared by 1942, and youth and women were drawn into the labour market to meet the urgent demand. Now, as Coulter relates in a different study, the concerns of adults over youth became the opposite of what they had been in the 1930s. Youth were now seen as too independent because they could earn wages at an early age. There was concern that youth were sacrificing their schooling for the short-term gain of war work in "blind-alley" occupations. Delinquency was now said to result not from idleness but from having "money to burn." There was special concern about girls' sexuality now that they had incomes and could evade the control of their parents.[46]

Quickly the average marriage age began to drop. During the early 1940s, as conscription was being debated and young people were drawn into the labour market in large numbers, the prospect facing single men of being drafted into the armed forces and sent overseas to battle prompted many of them to marry. Average age at marriage spiked downward in 1941 and continued to decline for the next twenty-five years.[47]

><><

Between 1850 and 1945 Canadian society had changed dramatically. Central to these changes for young people were the growth of the education system and the emergence of the labour market as the main source of livelihood. A century earlier most young people had had a rural base. Even if they earned some or all of their incomes off the farm, most had that base to fall back on when jobs dried up. In towns, many young men had been able to establish livelihoods by taking up an independent trade. By the middle of the twentieth century, these bases of independence had largely disappeared. Most young people — young men and growing numbers of young women — now achieved adult status by earning wages in the labour market.

The labour market presented both opportunities and risks. In times of growth and prosperity, the industrial economy offered higher incomes and standards of living, but it was notoriously hazardous. In his classic 1944 work *The Great Transformation*, political economist Karl Polanyi described the construction of the labour market in nineteenth-century Britain.[48] He observed that for the industrial economy to function, labour had to be treated as a commodity, responding to price signals. But, he noted, human labour is a fictitious commodity. Labour enters the market for reasons quite different from those of real commodities, and it depends on the labour market to sustain its physical existence. Its supply, moreover, is relatively inelastic; it is not in a position to reduce itself or to wait for more favourable opportunities. Polanyi concluded: "To allow the market mechanism to be the sole director of the fate of human beings and their natural environment, indeed, even of the amount and use of purchasing power, would result in the demolition of society."[49]

Writing in the wake of the catastrophic Great Depression, Polanyi had few to contradict him. It was clear to all that something fundamental had gone wrong with the market economy in the 1930s and that it would be foolhardy to depend upon it exclusively in the future. The response of the state to the particular problems of youth had been to fall back on education and training schemes and hope for the best. Young people knew through their experience that this strategy was inadequate. In the aftermath of the Depression and the war, young people expected the state to play a much greater role in minimizing the risks and expanding the opportunities for youth, ensuring that they would be treated as more than commodities by their society. The response in the postwar period would be the construction of the welfare state.

3 From Golden Age to Risk Society: The Postwar World

"The demonstration of the potentialities of the Canadian economy has been one of the outstanding features of the past five years," declared the Canadian government in its *Green Book on Reconstruction* in 1945. The rapid reversal of economic stagnation and mass unemployment brought about by the war effort had shown that governments could, when moved to do so, lead the country to prosperity. During the war years several major studies had developed plans for doing just that, driven by an overwhelming popular desire never to repeat the experiences of the Great Depression.[1]

Surveys of youth attitudes carried out by the Canadian Youth Commission during the war showed that young people wanted fundamental changes in social and labour-market policy. The Commission, an independent organization initiated by the YMCA with broad representation from Canada's regions, linguistic groups, religious faiths, unions, farmers, business, and government, used a combination of quantitative polling, in-depth interviewing, and youth conferences to survey youth attitudes on family, religion, recreation, health, education, and jobs. Its series of reports published after the war were among the first serious efforts ever made to canvass the views of Canadian youth.[2]

The surveys found widespread concerns among youth about access to education, good jobs, and social security. Young people anticipated the return of veterans at the end of the war and were concerned that their prospects in the job market would decline. Four out of five youth supported the principle of government intervention in the economy to ensure full employment, and nine out of ten believed that "government should make it possible for all young people who have the ability, but not the money, to go to university." Close to half of all youth reported that for financial reasons they had been forced to leave school early.

Youth were not alone. Unions, which had grown stronger during the late 1930s and the war years, were pressing for governments to promote full employment and income security and to strengthen the rights of workers to organize for better wages and benefits. Voters had shown the popularity of this direction with increasing support for a social-democratic party, the Co-operative Commonwealth Federation (CCF). The party's Regina Manifesto of 1933 had called for a stronger government role in the economy through the nationalization of key industries and the establishment of a welfare state with universal pensions, health and welfare insurance, children's allowances, unemployment insurance, and workers' compensation. In 1943 the CCF topped a national Gallup poll and came second in the Ontario elections. The following year it came to power in Saskatchewan, and in 1945 it elected twenty-eight members to the House of Commons.

The response of Mackenzie King's Liberal government to the broad popular demand for change in the postwar period has been called Canada's "Second National Policy."[3] John A. Macdonald and his Conservative Party had built the first National Policy around railways, tariffs, and immigration. Mackenzie King and his Liberal successors were the main architects of the second policy, and their materials were primarily macroeconomic, social, and labour-market mechanisms. Using Keynesian principles, Canadian governments aimed to sustain demand in the economy. Fiscal and monetary policies were to smooth the peaks and valleys of the business cycle and prevent any repeat of the disastrous collapse of the 1930s. At the same time, governments created a more favourable environment for workers to form unions and to bargain collectively with employers for wages and benefits. The aim was to make the labour market the main source of security for most people. To complement this policy, federal and provincial governments co-operated to develop a social safety net to protect those who could not support themselves in the labour market due to unemployment, disability, sickness, or old age.

All of this was done slowly, in piecemeal fashion, over more than a quarter-century. Even at its high point, in the early 1970s, Canada had a relatively meagre welfare state by international standards. It compared favourably only to the United States, primarily because of its system of universal public health care and affordable postsecondary education. Gosta Esping-Andersen, a Danish sociologist, has classed Canada as a liberal welfare state, in that it aimed to interfere minimally with the operation of the labour market. He contrasts the liberal regimes of Canada, the United States, Australia, New Zealand, and the United Kingdom with more developed corporatist welfare states in continental Europe and social-democratic regimes in Scandinavia. The Scandinavians go furthest in decommodifying labour, that is, providing benefits to people as citizens, regardless of their status in the labour market. Liberal regimes tend to rely primarily on the labour market to provide not only wages but also other benefits such as health and disability insurance and pensions. In a liberal regime these benefits are normally negotiated in collective agreements and delivered by private companies. Moreover, some of Canada's most important public schemes, such as unemployment insurance and the Canada and Quebec pension plans, are financed from the contributions of workers and their employers and paid out only to those who have contributed through their labour-market participation.[4]

Nevertheless, a liberal welfare state worked reasonably well in the prosperous quarter-century following the war — the so-called "golden age." Unemployment fluctuated between 3 and 7 per cent, and incomes rose rapidly. The labour market provided a reasonably good base of security for most people. The main problems were the chronically high rates of unemployment in certain regions, especially Atlantic Canada, and the evolution of a dual labour market. Workers in the primary labour market held secure jobs and had the protection of collective agreements or the favourable personnel policies of their employers. The jobs provided good wages, benefits, and working conditions. But parallel to this was a secondary labour market with none of those advantages. Here jobs were not merely on the low-skilled, low-paid bottom rung of a job ladder; they were qualitatively different from jobs in the primary labour market. They lacked career paths, training programs, job security, or benefits packages. This workforce was made up primarily of students and other young people, women, and racial or ethnic minorities.[5]

A distinctive youth labour market took shape during the golden age. Youth accounted for a small share of employment and a large share of unemployment. As students, young people typically found work in the secondary labour market, with its three major sources of jobs. The first was large secondary firms, such as security businesses, grocery stores, cleaning services, and construction companies. These paid minimum wages and hired young people for unskilled jobs that were often part-time, temporary, or summer employment. The second source of work was small businesses, "mom and pop" stores, such as bakeries, newsstands, restaurants, gas stations, and convenience stores. Examples in the rural economy include farm labour, wood cutting, and other menial tasks in primary production. This was low-paid casual work without a future but with little of the bitterness in personal relationships, supervision, and working conditions found in the first category. Such jobs were almost always found through personal contacts and were often one-off opportunities. The third source was under the table or off the books work, jobs not reported to the tax authorities, including babysitting, shovelling snow, painting houses, repairing cars, and some construction. Most of it was neighbourhood-based and generally found through family and friends.

Male working-class youth worked in the secondary labour market as students and, typically, for a few years after leaving school.[6] They then moved on to find work in the primary labour market, where the employers were typically large enterprises with unionized workplaces, good benefits packages, training programs, and clear career paths. Young working-class men rarely saw their first job as a step on a career path. They tended to have high quit rates — that is, they left their jobs with greater frequency than did older workers. As they grew older, various social factors, particularly marriage and peer pressure, led them to become more stable. This behaviour biased employers in the primary labour market against youth and led to hiring practices that tended to discriminate against them.

Employers judged job applicants by their attitudes, maturity, stability, and reliability. Specific skills, they believed, could be taught on the job if the worker had the right attitude. Indeed, most firms in the primary labour market did not put great emphasis on skills because they preferred to train entrants in their own methods. This tendency varied by industry. If skills learned in another job were important to the work process, they might be a factor in the hiring decision. More frequently, experience in a similar job was more important as a proxy for maturity and stability. The majority of youths hired into primary jobs did not know how to do the job they were hired for when they were hired.

Because of these firms' investment in the training period, both employer and employee had an incentive to maintain a stable relationship. Internal labour markets promoted this stability; the worker moved up through the firm, acquiring more skills and advancing as openings became available.

The golden age was the heyday of the unionized, male, blue-collar worker. As productivity increased in the 1950s and 1960s, and as collective bargaining became the normal practice for establishing wages, benefits, and working conditions, standards of living rose rapidly. For the first time large numbers of working-class people achieved what were thought to be middle-class incomes. Income inequality decreased in the society at large. Young people, it was assumed, would do even better than their parents. One U.S. study found that a young man who left home at age eighteen in the 1950s would, by age thirty, earn about 15 per cent more than his father had been earning when the young man was living at home.[7]

>o<

As the economy expanded, so too did the welfare state. A wide range of new jobs began to open up in the broader public sector. Many of these were well-paying professional and technical occupations in health, education, social welfare, and the civil service. The service sector of the economy began to come to the fore as the main source of new jobs during the 1960s, eclipsing the male-dominated goods-producing sector. Growing numbers of married women entered the labour force, many of them moving into these public-sector jobs, especially as teachers. The education system grew rapidly, in part because of the large group of baby-boomers who began entering it in the 1950s but also because of the rising expectations of youth and their parents as well as a growing demand from both the private and public sectors for increasing numbers of professional and technical workers.

In the 1940s the Canadian Youth Commission had found that many young people looked to the education system to prepare them for making a living, but their views reflected some of the contradictions that still appear in debates about education today. On the one hand, over half were critical of the failure of schools to prepare them for making a living, and only 51 per cent thought schools were doing a good job of guiding them to choose suitable occupations. On the other hand, most believed that the main purpose of schooling was not job preparation. The most important goal of education in their view was learning to think clearly about the problems of life and modern society. They rated the most important subjects they learned in school to be their first language and mathematics. They wanted instruction in sex, marriage, and home relationships on the curriculum. And although it was a lower priority overall, many also wanted to learn job-relevant skills in school. Young women in particular rated commercial studies as a high priority. Young men seemed less concerned about job preparation in school and about having to leave school, probably because of the easier access they had to the labour market, especially in blue-collar jobs. These findings are an early indicator of the trend towards increasingly higher levels of participation in education by women than men, at both secondary and postsecondary levels.

Studies commissioned by the Canadian Education Association between 1947 and 1951 examined high-school dropout rates (59 per cent of boys and 51 per cent of girls did not complete high school), the provision of "practical training," and the issue of whether young people were "adjusting satisfactorily in their post-school careers."[8] The CEA had two broad concerns. It wanted education to contribute to the employability of youth and to the supply of necessary skills in the expanding economy. At the same time it wanted to promote greater equity of access to education across social classes. These twin goals ran through discussions of education during the 1950s and 1960s. In the early postwar years, however, there was little inkling of the revolutionary changes coming in gender roles. The CEA reports recommended that the high-school curriculum include a variety of practical subjects geared to the different life prospects of boys and girls. In addition to a core of academic subjects, they recommended courses for boys in business topics, shop work, agricultural science and practice, and farm mechanics and for girls in business training, home economics, home nursing, and child care.[9]

In the early 1960s the concept of "human capital" appeared.[10] Economists held that higher levels of educational attainment would increase the skills of the workforce and serve to expand the production frontier of the economy, increasing prosperity for all. The result was a period of heavy investment in all levels of the education system. The federal and provincial governments financed the rapid expansion of universities and the creation of an entire new layer of vocationally oriented postsecondary education in community colleges. The driving force behind this expansion was a growing demand in the labour market for workers with postsecondary education and training, but a large part of the rationale for the high levels of public expenditure on education in the 1960s also revolved around the promotion of social equity. Individuals of all social classes were to have access to education, and their increased levels of skill would contribute to ever-increasing productivity as well as greater equality of opportunity. According to the theory, the investment in human capital would pay off in the growth of good jobs.

The underside of this rosy picture displayed a growing level of alienation among youth of the baby-boom generation. During the late 1950s and 1960s transitions from school to work were not much of a concern; in most years plenty of jobs were available for all. But the nature of the work left many young people without much enthusiasm and frequently with open antipathy. Many blue-collar workers found themselves carrying out the boring, repetitive, assembly-line tasks dictated by the principles of scientific management. Professional and technical staff felt pressure to conform to stifling norms of behaviour and attitude, well documented in William Whyte's 1956 book *The Organization Man*.[11] The response from many youth was a retreat into youth subcultures — the beat generation, hippies, and the student protest movement — and a rejection of the dominant culture. "There is 'nearly full employment,' " U.S. educator Paul Goodman wrote in his 1960 landmark book, *Growing up Absurd*, "but there get to be fewer jobs that are necessary or unquestionably useful; that require energy and draw on some of one's best capacities; and that can be done keeping one's honor and dignity."

> I often ask [youth], "What do you want to work at? If you have the chance. When you get out of school, college, the service, etc." ... I remember talking to half a dozen young fellows at Van Wagner's Beach outside of Hamilton, Ontario; and all of them had this one thing to say: "Nothing." They didn't believe that what to work at was the kind of thing one *wanted*. They rather expected that two or three of them would work for the electric company in town, but they couldn't care less. I turned away from the conversation abruptly because of the uncontrollable burning tears in my eyes and constriction in my chest. Not feeling sorry for them, but tears of frank dismay for the waste of our humanity (they were nice kids).[12]

During the 1960s, the U.S. psychologist Erik H. Erikson elaborated further on a concept of adolescence originally pioneered by his fellow countryman G. Stanley Hall, a psychologist and educationist. Erikson defined adolescence as a period in which the main challenge was to consolidate an individual ego identity, a task that often demanded a moratorium from the lock-step progression through school and into a job. For middle-class youth, the moratorium might involve time out for experimentation with a variety of identities — immersion in a youth subculture, a footloose year or two travelling in Europe and the Middle East, or a volunteer job with CUSO. Working-class youth who did not have these options might drift through a number of low-paying jobs in the secondary labour market with little concern about the future, focused more on adventure and disposable income.[13] But until the 1970s few young people worried about the availability of well-paying career jobs once they decided to settle down.

The arrival of the baby-boom generation in the labour market from the mid-1960s to the mid-1980s coincided with a gathering crisis of the Canadian economy and its welfare state, part of a broader international trend. In the late 1960s the rate of productivity growth in the economies of all the Western industrialized countries slowed down. Using their Keynesian tools, governments tried to sustain demand and economic growth, which only brought on the age of "stagflation" — high inflation and little growth. At the same time the large U.S.-based multinational corporations that had dominated global production and markets since the 1940s began to encounter a challenge to their hegemony from competitors in Europe and Japan. A new era of global competition had begun. By the early 1970s the large corporations were beginning to experience declining profits.[14] By one account, profit rates in the industrialized capitalist world dropped by 50 to 60 per cent between the 1960s and the 1980s.[15]

To make adjustments, firms from all major industrial countries began to adopt new strategies, which fell into three main areas. Some companies, particularly in the industries that used scientific management in their labour processes, began to shift production to low-wage countries, especially in Asia and Latin America. The great advantage of scientific management was that it allowed unskilled and semi-skilled workers to be trained quickly and easily to perform their assigned functions. Soon everything from shoes, clothes, and electronic consumer goods to semiconductors, machine tools, steel, and automobiles was being made in low-wage countries and shipped to markets in high-wage countries.

A second key strategy was the introduction of new, computer-based technology that reduced the need for labour, particularly the semi-skilled, high-wage, blue-collar, unionized labour force that had predominated in the main industries of the industrialized countries. This workforce was reduced, and greater reliance was placed on smaller numbers of highly skilled technicians and professionals and their new technologies. This shift had a strong impact on employment in the manufacturing industries of all the industrialized countries. For example, between 1970 and 1993, manufacturing output doubled in the United States while employment in that sector fell by as much as 10 per cent.[16] The productivity of manufacturing workers increased enormously, but there were now far fewer of them, and the displaced workers were not able to achieve the same high levels of productivity in their new occupations, which were primarily in the service industries.

In Canada technological innovation also depressed the value of primary products. By the mid-1980s the prices of foods, forest products, metals, and minerals had reached their lowest levels in history relative to manufactured products. In general industrial production was becoming less material-intensive. Innovations in microelectronics, biotechnology, and materials science meant that a higher proportion of the value added to products was now derived from knowledge-based, high-tech inputs than from raw materials.[17] This development forced widespread restructuring in Canada's resource industries, with a resulting downswing in employment.

As the need for workers in the goods-producing industries declined, the service sector became the only part of the economy with significant new job creation. By the mid-1980s this situation was having a major social impact. Well-paid, unionized blue-collar jobs became scarcer, while new job creation clustered around two poles: the skilled technical and professional jobs of both the service and goods-producing sectors; and the low-skilled McJobs of the traditional service industries — cashiers, sales clerks, security guards, and food-counter attendants, for instance. In Canada this labour-market polarization was described in a landmark study, *Good Jobs, Bad Jobs*, published by the Economic Council of Canada in 1990.[18] Looking ahead to the year 2000, the Canadian government projected that net job growth would be greatest for occupations requiring more than sixteen years of education and training; 45 per cent of new jobs were expected to fall into this category. During the same period, however, about one-third of new jobs were expected to require less than twelve years of education.[19] Jobs in the middle — those requiring between twelve and sixteen years of education — were in decline.

The third key strategy of employers, both private and public, was to seek greater flexibility from their workers. The trend since the 1970s has been to "downsize" and "delayer" the number of permanent employees to a smaller core in order to cut the costs associated with regular salaries, benefits, and severance provisions. The employer then hires additional workers on a part-time, temporary, or "just-in-time" basis to meet its needs as they arise, or the employer may contract out the supply of certain services or goods to other firms. A firm might persuade highly skilled professionals to join its core staff by offering performance bonuses and stock options, or it might employ high-priced consultants. Other workers lose the protection of employment contracts and collective agreements and in turn receive lower wages and have less job security.[20]

As this crisis gathered force in the industrialized countries during the 1970s and 1980s, pressure came to bear on the Keynesian welfare state. Deficit-spending did not seem to revive the economy, but only fuelled inflation and fed growing government debt. In time it came to be blamed for the crisis itself. Voters turned to conservative parties, such as those of Margaret Thatcher in Britain and Ronald Reagan in the United States, parties committed to an ideology of neo-liberalism, that is, to reducing the role of the activist state in the economy and replacing it with free-market solutions.[21] Governments began to privatize the enterprises they owned as well as many of the services previously considered to be public goods. Henceforth market forces would determine which goods and services were to be produced. Governments were to eliminate their deficits and reduce their levels of public debt. This would contribute to lower taxes, lower interest rates, and a better climate for investment by the private sector.

Ironically, some of the early advocates of neo-liberalism — especially the Reagan administration in the United States and the Mulroney government in Canada — presided over unprecedented levels of government deficit and additions to the public debt. In Canada this condition was largely due to the high interest-rate policy of the Bank of Canada as it aimed to reduce the inflation rate to zero. It was left to the Liberals, elected in 1993 under Jean Chrétien, with Paul Martin as finance minister — more committed neo-liberals than the Conservatives had been — to bring the deficits down.

Government agendas dropped the policy of full employment, or even of "high and stable levels of employment," a central goal of the Keynesian welfare state, replacing it with the concept of the Non-Accelerating Inflation Rate of Unemployment (NAIRU), the rate of unemployment that would not trigger inflation. The consensus in Canada's Department of Finance was that this rate stood at somewhere between 5 and 8 per cent. In a time of economic growth, as the unemployment rate declined towards the NAIRU, the Bank of Canada had to "step on the brakes" by increasing interest rates. This move would restrict the money supply, thus slowing new investment and job creation. Apologists argued that it was simply a monetary policy and that its influence on employment was only a side-effect. In practice, some people remained or became unemployed, while many others were insecure enough to restrain their wage demands and spending. The method was analogous to a decision about where to locate an expressway or a nuclear waste collective agreements and in turn receive lower wages and have less job security.[20]

As this crisis gathered force in the industrialized countries during the 1970s and 1980s, pressure came to bear on the Keynesian welfare state. Deficit-spending did not seem to revive the economy, but only fuelled inflation and fed growing government debt. In time it came to be blamed for the crisis itself. Voters turned to conservative parties, such as those of Margaret Thatcher in Britain and Ronald Reagan in the United States, parties committed to an ideology of neo-liberalism, that is, to reducing the role of the activist state in the economy and replacing it with free-market solutions.[21] Governments began to privatize the enterprises they owned as well as many of the services previously considered to be public goods. Henceforth market forces would determine which goods and services were to be produced. Governments were to eliminate their deficits and reduce their levels of public debt. This would contribute to lower taxes, lower interest rates, and a better climate for investment by the private sector.

Ironically, some of the early advocates of neo-liberalism — especially the Reagan administration in the United States and the Mulroney government in Canada — presided over unprecedented levels of government deficit and additions to the public debt. In Canada this condition was largely due to the high interest-rate policy of the Bank of Canada as it aimed to reduce the inflation rate to zero. It was left to the Liberals, elected in 1993 under Jean Chrétien, with Paul Martin as finance minister — more committed neo-liberals than the Conservatives had been — to bring the deficits down.

Government agendas dropped the policy of full employment, or even of "high and stable levels of employment," a central goal of the Keynesian welfare state, replacing it with the concept of the Non-Accelerating Inflation Rate of Unemployment (NAIRU), the rate of unemployment that would not trigger inflation. The consensus in Canada's Department of Finance was that this rate stood at somewhere between 5 and 8 per cent. In a time of economic growth, as the unemployment rate declined towards the NAIRU, the Bank of Canada had to "step on the brakes" by increasing interest rates. This move would restrict the money supply, thus slowing new investment and job creation. Apologists argued that it was simply a monetary policy and that its influence on employment was only a side-effect. In practice, some people remained or became unemployed, while many others were insecure enough to restrain their wage demands and spending. The method was analogous to a decision about where to locate an expressway or a nuclear waste site: some people would inevitably lose out, but their sacrifice was viewed as necessary to the interests of society as a whole. In this case, there were no public hearings and very little control even by elected representatives, and the losers were always the same people, those most likely to be laid off in a downturn, and particularly the young.

Government programs to promote employment ran concurrently with these macroeconomic policies. But where the Keynesian approach had concentrated on demand-side management, the new approach focused on supply factors. The new role of the state was to promote the structural competitiveness of the nation's economy. It could do this in a variety of ways. Industrial policy encouraged innovation and technological upgrading or more aggressive international marketing, for example, through "Team Canada" trade missions to Asia and Latin America. Labour-market policy focused on education and skills training, one of the few ways in which governments could still respond to problems of unemployment and insecurity.

>o<

The problem of youth unemployment became a major social issue in the late 1970s and early 1980s, when late members of the baby-boom generation tried to enter the labour market during a time of economic stagnation, high inflation, and recession. Many of the themes of earlier periods re-emerged. The influential Dodge Report of 1981 recommended that education be geared more effectively to the demands of the labour market and that governments do more to facilitate the transition from school to work.[22] The goal of social equity through education receded, and more emphasis was placed on the efficiency of education programs and transition paths.

An important piece of youth research from this period was the Tri-City study, a survey that tracked the school-work transitions of a sample of high-school and university graduates in Edmonton, Sudbury, and Toronto from 1985 to 1989. In *Young Workers in the Service Economy*, a 1990 paper produced for the Economic Council of Canada, University of Alberta sociologists Harvey Krahn and Graham Lowe used the data from this survey to point out significant changes in the experiences of young Canadians in the labour market of the 1980s.[23]

They found that the labour-market participation rate of young people aged fifteen to twenty-four had risen from 56 per cent in 1966 to over 70 per cent by 1989. Statistics Canada figures showed this increase to be due to two main factors: the increasing participation rate of young women and the increasing number of students with part-time jobs.[24] At the same time a higher proportion of young people were staying in school after their high-school graduation. By the time of Krahn and Lowe's study the rate of enrolment in postsecondary education had climbed to 75.7 per cent of seventeen-year-olds, one of the highest rates among industrialized countries. More youth were staying in school longer or returning to school after a time in the labour force.

Krahn and Lowe observed a new pattern in the transition from school to work. The period of leaving the education system and entering the labour market was becoming more prolonged, and the route more circuitous. The growing labour-force activity of young people prior to leaving school, and the longer duration of time spent in school, blurred the boundaries between student and worker roles. The traditional sequence of completing a formal education and moving into continuous employment was giving way to a different situation in which education was prolonged and co-existed with employment. There was no single or even predominant pattern of labour-force entry for either high-school or university graduates. These diverse combinations of education and work distinguished graduates in the 1980s from those in earlier decades, when there had tended to be a clear point of passage from school to work.

Over 80 per cent of employed young people, both student and non-student, had jobs in the service sector of the economy, which accounted for almost all new jobs created during the 1980s. Instead of passing from a secondary to a primary labour-market segment upon leaving school, or instead of passing through a moratorium period, young people now entered a polarized labour market in which many of those with higher education went on to "good" jobs in professional and business services while large numbers remained trapped in the low-pay, low-status jobs of the secondary labour market, especially in the consumer-services labour-market segment. They took up jobs as sales clerks, food and beverage servers, cashiers and tellers, stock clerks, and sales supervisors — the work that came to be known as McJobs. Some young women did move out of the consumer-services segment and into other kinds of sales, clerical, and service jobs after graduating from high school, and some young men moved into blue-collar jobs, but almost 40 per cent of high-school graduates and about 9 per cent of university graduates were still working in the consumer-services segment two years after leaving school.

This situation was the result of changes in both the supply and the demand sides of the labour market. The number of young workers peaked in the early 1980s as the crest of the baby boom flowed through the fifteen to twenty-four age range, but the supply remained high throughout the decade for reasons other than simple population numbers. Young women were now choosing to enter the labour market in equal numbers with young men, and students of both sexes in their late teens were looking for jobs in greater numbers than ever before. At the same time the economic stagnation of the 1970s and the recession of the early 1980s choked off labour-market demand. The result was a downward displacement, as high-school graduates held on to their student jobs, blocking high-school students and those who had dropped out of high school from access to the service jobs of the student labour market. University graduates in turn, unable to find entry-level career jobs, held on to their service-sector and clerical jobs, displacing high-school graduates. The unemployment rates showed this clearly. The highest rates were found among those who had dropped out before completing a high-school diploma; at each higher level of educational attainment, the unemployment rate was less than it was for the education level below. This phenomenon led some to claim that employers were practising widespread credentialism, that is, hiring on the basis of educational qualifications regardless of the skill requirements of the job.[25]

Youth unemployment rates remained high through the 1980s despite the economic recovery. Many of those who had jobs remained stuck in the lower levels of the consumer-services segment of the job market, where underemployment and dissatisfaction were common. Krahn and Lowe called it an "involuntary moratorium." These underemployed youth were not using the skills they had learned in school, they were not working in the type of job to which they aspired, and they were experiencing a high degree of involuntary part-time work. Paradoxically, those with lower levels of formal education were the most likely to feel that their jobs did not make use of their knowledge and skills.

Krahn and Lowe observed that a degree or diploma would be required to open up further career options for most young people. Since a sizable minority of university graduates were also employed in consumer services, high-school graduates were not even next in line for higher-status service jobs. Moreover, employment prospects in manufacturing, construction, or traditionally better-paying blue-collar areas were decreasing. It appeared that many youths with only a high-school education would be trapped in lower-level jobs in consumer-service industries, if not unemployed. Social-class differences were likely to persist, they said, despite generally rising education levels, and they could be expected to continue even if the average level of education in the society increased. This was due to "a contradiction arising out of rapid growth

of low-skill jobs and rising educational attainment."[26] It was possible
that the shrinking size of the youth cohort of the labour force would
reduce or solve this problem, but it could not be assumed that higher
levels of education would change the pattern of polarization emerging
on the demand side of the labour market.

><

In the 1960s the average age of Canadians at first marriage dropped to
its lowest level ever — twenty-five for men, twenty-two for women.[27]
The high marriage rate and lower marriage age in the 1950s and 1960s
are often attributed to the good labour-market conditions and the security provided by welfare state programs. The growing availability of consumer credit also made it easier to set up a household. It is not as clear
why marriage rates have declined and average age at marriage has
increased again since that time. Beginning in 1973, they have quickly
returned to levels comparable to those of the Great Depression. By 1992
the average age at first marriage was twenty-nine for men and twenty-
seven for women. The percentage of people aged twenty to twenty-four
who were married declined from 42 per cent in 1971 to 9 per cent in
1996, and of those aged twenty-five to twenty-nine from 75 per cent in
1971 to 36 per cent in 1996.[28]

Unlike past decades, large numbers of young men and women are
choosing to live together in common-law unions, in some cases as a pro-
logue to marriage and in others as an alternative to it. The 1996 Census
of Canada shows that the number of common-law unions increased by
28 per cent from 1991 to 1996, a rate of growth sixteen times higher
than that of marriages in the same period. There is also a growing number of lone-parent families.[29] This suggests a situation quite different
from that of the Great Depression. We cannot conclude that young people are delaying marriage simply because of economic conditions.
Labour-market conditions may be one factor, but it seems unlikely that
it is the only one or even the main one. Rather, it seems more likely that
marriage is becoming detraditionalized and that Canadian society is see-
ing the emergence of a more diverse set of family arrangements.
Changes in gender roles and family structures may be as much a cause of
changes in the labour market as they are an effect.

Less committed relationships, a high incidence of unemployment
and involuntary part-time employment, difficulty gaining entry to career
jobs in the years following departure from the education system, low
incomes, and a threadbare social safety net: these are the dominating
facts of life that young people now encounter as they come of age in

Canada. In this world, youth are confronted with a complex set of decisions, each of them having major consequences for their lives. To a far greater degree than past generations, they bear individual responsibility for making these decisions. They may receive little or no counselling or advice in doing so, and what they do receive may be incomplete or erroneous. The world may appear to be their oyster as they contemplate the full range of alternative lives arrayed before them, but they are, paradoxically, firmly bound by the necessity to make good choices in the education system and then to find their way into the labour market. Failure to do so is at their own risk.

4

Education
and Changing
Aspirations

*G*randy's River Collegiate serves the fishing outports of Burnt Islands and Rose Blanche in southwestern Newfoundland. About 250 students attend, and 40 to 50 graduate each year. Most of the parents of these students never completed high school. There seemed to be little point. Once they reached school-leaving age, they could go to work in the fishery and begin earning an adult's wages on a fishing boat or in the fish plant. They needed specialized skills to do these jobs, but school was not the place to learn them. Those who did complete high school often left the community for more education and a career elsewhere.

But since the collapse of the cod fishery these communities have had high unemployment, and they have been dependent on government support. Now almost all students finish their diplomas, and two-thirds of the graduates go on to postsecondary studies. "I know one thing," one student said, "if there were jobs here now and I knew I could get out of school and get a job, I'd be gone tomorrow. . . . Now there's nothing out there. There's no other choice but to get an education, so that's why I'm going to do it."[1]

Throughout Eastern Canada's rural communities the story is much the same. In "Rockland," the pseudonym researchers have given to an isolated rural county in Nova Scotia, fish-processing and forestry are the main occupations. In the 1986 census, only 30 per cent of the adults in the county reported that they had graduated from high school. Yet the Rockland study found that very few of the students in the county now drop out before finishing Grade 12. In fact, Rockland's dropout rate is one of the lowest in Nova Scotia. When researchers asked why this was so they found that the abysmal local job market was the one obvious factor. There was almost nothing for young people to do in the traditional economy. The county had been gradually depopulated as both fish-processing and forestry became limited by sharply reduced quotas. The fish-processing plant had not hired new workers in several years and was forced to lay off several hundred of its experienced workers, who then had first claim on any new jobs that might open up. In forestry the only option was providing logs to a pulp mill in the neighbouring county, which would have required a large investment in equipment.[2]

The rapid change in the prospects of youth in these kinds of small towns and rural communities has been dramatic. These youth seldom believe that education will help them contribute to the revitalization of their community's economy. It seems that it will take far more than well-schooled young people to do that. Rather, they see education as a means of escape, a ticket to a life elsewhere. That elsewhere, it turns out, is a province, a country, and a world full of other young people preparing themselves to compete for good jobs and incomes in the labour market. The pressure to complete high school and go on to post-secondary studies in the larger centres of Canada is just as strong as it is in the Newfoundland outports. Whether they like school or hate it, Canadian youth understand that they need the knowledge and skills — or at least the credentials — that education can provide if they hope to have an interesting job, a good income, and a comfortable standard of living as adults.

Across Canada young people intend to go further in school than their parents did, and a majority of them hope to have careers in professional or management occupations. By the time they reach the age of twenty-four, 85 per cent of youth have completed a high-school diploma and 72 per cent have undertaken postsecondary studies of some kind, although only 35 per cent have actually completed a degree, diploma, or certificate by that age. These statistics represent a major increase in educational attainment from over a generation ago. In the 1950s less than half of the country's youth completed a high-school diploma, and as recently as 1980 the rate of high-school completion was only 70 per cent.[3]

Another way to look at this trend is to consider what youth are doing at various ages. In 1995-96, 82 per cent of seventeen-year-old Canadians were still in school full-time, at either the secondary or post-secondary level, compared to 70 per cent in 1980. Some 38 per cent of youth aged eighteen to twenty-one were attending a postsecondary pro-gram, either full-time or part-time, compared to 26 per cent in 1985. This was the highest rate of participation in postsecondary education for that age group of any industrialized country. Moving up the age range, the rate of participation in postsecondary education of those aged twenty-two to twenty-five increased from 10 per cent to 23 per cent between 1985 and 1994, and from 3 per cent to 10 per cent for those aged twenty-six to twenty-nine in the same period.[4]

Canada's high rate of educational achievement is one of the main reasons that it has been ranked at the top of the United Nations' Human Development Index for the past several years. Canadians invest a lot in education, both as individuals and through their taxes: about 7.6 per cent of Gross Domestic Product in 1993, the highest rate among the G7 countries.[5]

Surprisingly, there has been very little direct research into what is motivating Canadian youth to stay in school longer, perhaps because Canadians have so little doubt about the value of education. The Tri-City study of the 1980s did ask this question and found that two-thirds of those planning further education gave career-related reasons for doing so. The responses included "to get a job," "to have a career," "to have a higher standard of living," "to be independent," and "to get ahead." In distant second place, at about 18 per cent, were responses that valued education for its own sake. These came from youth who "enjoy school" or want "more knowledge" or "more skills" — motives certainly not incompatible with career-related reasons. Only a small per-centage gave more passive statements, such as "my parents want me to," "my friends are going," "it's something to do," or "the social life." "These results," the researchers concluded, "show very clearly how much young Canadians are committed to the belief that higher educa-tion is the ticket to career success."[6]

Educational aspirations, in other words, are closely related to career aspirations. This point may seem obvious, but it is critical. Youth are staying in school longer because they see it as the key to their future careers and living standards. And career aspirations are also high. A sub-sample of the Tri-City study, for example, found that almost three-quar-ters of graduating high-school students in Edmonton aspired to professional or managerial occupations, jobs that made up less than one-quarter of the Canadian labour force.[7]

During the early 1990s, when recession had put an end to the boom of the mid-1980s to late 1980s, large numbers of young people withdrew from the labour market. Attendance at school, both secondary and postsecondary, increased to record levels. The trend is not surprising, for almost all youth were receiving — and continue to receive — a consistent message from parents, governments, and employers: stay in school.

><<

Does more education mean more opportunity? Let's begin with the changing aspirations of women. Almost all young women now intend to have lifetime careers in the labour market. This was true of large numbers of women of the baby-boom generation, but it is now an almost universal phenomenon. More women than men complete high school and more undertake postsecondary studies, and their reasons for doing so are no different than those of their male counterparts. Almost all young people expect to work outside the home, whether as employees or in a business of their own, throughout their adult lives.[8]

Yet there are major differences in how young women and young men view their prospective careers in relation to other adult roles. Dianne Looker, a professor of sociology at Acadia University, has studied the evolution of the attitudes and career plans of a large sample of youth in Nova Scotia who were aged seventeen in 1989. She found that the plans of young men and women for working in the paid labour force are almost identical when they look ahead to the times after leaving school that are "before marriage" and "after marriage before children." But the plans diverge at that point. Less than two-thirds of young women plan to work outside the home as parents of preschoolers and, of these, less than one-third plan to work full-time. Almost all young women plan to return to the labour force once their children are in school; three-quarters of them intend to do this on a full-time basis. Looking ahead to the "empty-nest" phase of their lives, the career plans of young women and young men are again virtually identical.[9]

Looker noted that young women now view marriage and parenthood as "career contingencies." They anticipate these contingencies, but they have not yet resolved the conflict those plans will create. Although young men and women generally agree on the principle of sexual equality, they still tend to have traditional views of their roles in the domestic sphere. Young men believe that parenthood means they will have to have a job; young women believe it means they will have to stay at home. Yet both plan to have careers in the labour market. This puts much more pressure on young women to develop strategies that will allow them to achieve both goals.

This profound change in the attitudes to work and career plans of young women is central to the social changes of our time. Since the 1960s, increasing numbers of women have rejected the isolation and dependence experienced in being confined to domestic work. Very few young women could find meaning in their lives without the challenge of a career. If affordable child care were more accessible in Canada, the percentage of women who plan to work when they have young children would probably rise substantially.

Still, most young women prefer to devote time to raising their children but feel compelled to work, at least on a part-time basis, because of the difficulty a family experiences in earning sufficient income from one person's wages. In 1997 Statistics Canada reported that most families needed two incomes to meet their consumption needs.[10] Its study of households with two adult partners, married or common-law, found that 60.5 per cent relied on income from both partners to meet household needs. Some thirty years earlier only a third of such households relied on income from both partners. This situation has come about as a result of both declining real incomes and increasing consumption norms.

In the late nineteenth and early twentieth centuries, one of the key struggles of male workers was for a family wage, a level of income that would allow the male breadwinner to support his wife and children. Most women did not work outside the home after marriage unless their husbands' wages were inadequate for family survival. This practice was reinforced by the "marriage bar" — the policy of many employers requiring that women leave employment when they married; in some places this requirement was enshrined in legislation. In our own time we have seen the demise of the concept of the family wage, partly as a cause and partly as an effect of the large-scale entry of women into the labour force. Moreover, with half of all marriages expected to end in divorce and more couples living together in less committed relationships, young women need to plan for their own independence.[11]

In short, for a variety of reasons it has now become the norm for young women to plan to have lifetime careers in the labour market. This has meant a radical change in their life course patterns, with many implications both for themselves and for young men, as well as for the labour market.

>o<

Some 15 per cent of young Canadians do not complete high school. For many years the dropout rate was estimated at double this percentage, and much consternation was expressed at the "cost to Canada" of this waste of human resources. In 1992 the business-oriented Conference Board of Canada issued a report, *Dropping Out: The Cost to Canada*, in which it calculated that those who left school prematurely in 1989 alone would cost Canada $4 billion in lost earnings, taxes, and social-service expenditures over their lifetimes.[12] Other major reports of the late 1980s and early 1990s drew similar conclusions, pointing to the need for more skilled workers in the new knowledge economy and the threat to Canada's competitiveness from weaknesses in the education system, including its high dropout rate.[13]

Several assumptions in these reports need to be questioned, beginning with their estimates of the dropout rate itself. The Conference Board assumed the dropout rate to be 30 per cent, but the most authoritative estimate of the dropout rate found that although some students leave the education system in their teens, many return and complete their diplomas after a time away from school.[14] Of Canadians aged twenty-two to twenty-four in 1995, 85 per cent had completed a high-school diploma. Moreover, almost a quarter of those who did not complete a high-school diploma did undertake some form of further education or training towards a postsecondary qualification, mainly in the skilled trades.

It is also a dubious assumption that a 100 per cent high-school completion rate would prevent the lost income, lost taxes, and higher social-service expenditures projected by the Conference Board. There is already considerable underemployment among those with high-school diplomas and postsecondary qualifications. It is, at best, an unproven assumption that higher educational qualifications in the population summon forth better jobs, at least in anything less than the long run.

It is undeniable, however, that those who fail to complete a high-school diploma face a major disadvantage when they enter the labour market. It is important, therefore, to ask who tends to drop out, and why. Fortunately, a good deal of research has been done on this topic over the last decade.[15]

Young men are more likely to drop out of high school than young women. Recent figures show the high-school dropout rate nationally as 19 per cent for men and 11 per cent for women, for an average of 15 per cent. The rate is over 20 per cent for young men in Newfoundland, Prince Edward Island, Quebec, and Manitoba. Although it is declining everywhere, dropping out is still more common in rural areas.[16]

Dropout rates are higher for students who come from low-income families, whose parents have low levels of education and negative attitudes towards education, who come from single-parent or no-parent households, who marry or have children at an early age, or who are disabled. Aboriginal youth are also less likely than others to complete a high-school diploma. The risk of dropping out increases significantly when these characteristics are combined to form a pattern that has been called "cumulative disadvantage." These characteristics, though, are not in themselves *causes* of dropping out. Sid Gilbert and his colleagues, after analysing the results of the 1991 School Leavers Survey, identified a set of characteristics that combined to define a high-risk group — most of the characteristics mentioned above — yet almost three-quarters of this group nevertheless succeeded in completing a high-school diploma.[17]

Many factors play a role in dropping out, especially the qualities of the school environment and the teaching. When students who drop out are asked for their reasons, the most common response is dislike of the school, especially boredom with the curriculum and inability to see how their studies relate to their current or future lives. This may explain why dropping out is more common in rural areas, where the connection between the curriculum and real life is often less than apparent. The alienation increases when academic performances are weak, when students are streamed into terminal programs, or when they are treated in a hostile manner by the school authorities. The process is self-reinforcing, and gradually the young person disengages emotionally, psychologically, and finally physically.

Some youth say they dropped out to take a job, but this is really the other side of the same coin. Few young people are forced to drop out of school for financial reasons. Alienation from school is the push factor; a job is the alternative, the pull factor that makes leaving school a real possibility. Between two-thirds and three-quarters of all young people who drop out of school report some combination of these reasons. Many of them add that, from their perspective, leaving school was not entirely voluntary. Either they felt pressure from school authorities to leave, or they were expelled outright.

The remaining one-quarter to one-third of students leave school for a variety of other reasons. Various personal situations predominate, including pregnancy, marriage, or problems in their home. Dropping out, then, is often part of an abrupt experience of coming of age. It is common for early leavers to move into traditional adult gender roles when they drop out: men into the labour market and women into domestic roles.[18]

In their attitudes, early leavers are not very different from those who stay in school. It is common for high-school students to find the curriculum boring, to be alienated by school rules and the experience of being streamed, and to react to authoritarian attitudes of teachers. Many stay in school but rebel against it by unruly behaviour or skipping classes. Journalist Sandro Contenta describes this eloquently in his book *Rituals of Failure.*

> At the end of the week, on sunny spring days, schools are like pots of sim-mering water with teachers sitting on the lids. By late in the afternoon the risk of boiling over is great. We can perhaps blame this delicate state of affairs on the impertinence of sunshine. For students bored out of their minds, the pull of the outside is irresistible. I've been in schools, Coal Harbour in Nova Scotia, for example, where the steam escapes with a rush and whole classes are cancelled because students simply don't show up. And it's not as though they skip class and disappear. They usually just hang out around the school, shooting the breeze, virtually unaware of their own defiance. There are few instances when revolt is so spontaneous and natural.[19]

Yet both those who leave and those who stay tend to agree that educa-tion is important. Both accept as a fact of life that educational qualifica-tions are the key to success in the labour market, and very few question that this is as it should be.

In this respect, Canadian youth are very different from the young British working-class males described by Paul Willis in his book *Learn-ing to Labour: How Working Class Kids Get Working Class Jobs.* Willis found that his group of working-class students rejected the whole idea of schooling as a way to earn credentials that would move them from working-class to middle-class occupations, incomes, and status. They behaved like the members of a proud, alien culture, rejecting school rules, academic pursuits, and teachers' authority. They valued the work and culture of their fathers, based in manual occupations and male camaraderie, and they chose those occupations when they left school.[20]

Most Canadian youth, by contrast, do not have a strong alternative culture of this kind to serve as an option to mainstream, middle-class definitions of success. Traditional working-class jobs are in decline, and low-paying, unskilled occupations have little appeal. Formal education is accepted as the necessary path for entry to good jobs with good incomes and status. Any exceptions that may once have existed — work in the primary sector in rural areas, or factory jobs in industrial centres — have dwindled in number and now offer few opportunities. The main destinations of youth without high-school diplomas are the McJobs of the consumer-service industries or unemployment. Canadian youth know this. (This may also be true in Britain by this time. In the years since Willis's book was published in 1977, most of the traditional entry-level jobs for working-class young men have disappeared.)

The only viable alternative to completing high school, and a route taken almost exclusively by males, is to learn a skilled trade through a combination of experience and apprenticeship or mature entry to a college program. About a quarter of young men who have not completed high school have gone in this direction by the age of twenty-four, and more may do so at a later age. But to date very few young women have ventured into the skilled trades, and most Canadian youth are not attracted by skilled blue-collar occupations, even though a reasonable number of such job opportunities appear to exist, with decent incomes in many of them.

The discovery that most early leavers value education led University of Toronto sociologist Julian Tanner to call them "reluctant rebels."[21] In their alienation they find little scope for creative protest or positive action. Their rebellion amounts to little more than self-selection to low-income futures in marginal jobs.

✕

Given current labour-market conditions, we could easily define dropping out as the failure to complete a postsecondary program. This tendency, too, is well understood by most Canadian youth. About four out of five high-school graduates now undertake further studies for a degree, diploma, or certificate, primarily at a university, by the time they are twenty-four years old.[22] Many of the high-school graduates who have not already done so could return to school in the future. As we did with the early leavers, however, it is worth asking why some decide not to continue their studies after completing their high-school diploma. Completing high school has been the minimum norm for perhaps fifty years now, but it is widely recognized that failure to complete a post-secondary program has become a source of disadvantage in the labour market. Who are the youth who decide not to continue, and what are their reasons for making this apparently irrational decision?

The pattern here is similar to that of the early leavers, and again family backgrounds have a strong influence on the aspirations of youth. Several status attainment studies conducted in the 1970s, when researchers were trying to determine if the expansion of postsecondary educational opportunities was doing anything to erode the structure of class privilege in Canada, found that the children of well-educated, high-income parents are much more likely to complete high-school and post-secondary education and go on to well-paying professional or managerial occupations.[23] It is less well understood why this is so. What, precisely, is the process by which expectations are transferred from parents to children, and how are these expectations translated into goals, strategies, and actions?

In 1990 Lesley Andres of the University of British Columbia conducted a series of in-depth interviews with students graduating from high school in Vancouver. She questioned human capital theory's assumption that individuals make rational decisions about postsecondary education based strictly upon considerations of the return on investment in their human capital. Her goal was to find out why some chose to continue on to postsecondary education while others did not. After a series of initial and follow-up interviews, she concluded that some youth simply had a "feel for the game" while others did not. Many said it was always assumed in their families that they would go on to university or college. This expectation was "internalized as second nature and forgotten as history," she writes, quoting French sociologist Pierre Bourdieu, whose "theory of practice" helps to explain how advantages are passed from generation to generation within the family as "social or cultural capital." This feel for the game led them to choose the right courses and aim for the grade-point averages that would ensure a successful passage from high school to postsecondary studies. Those who lacked this feel did not know how to play the game, or even that they had a place in it. They anticipated limited job opportunities and recognized that their chances would be greater with postsecondary studies, but they still believed that university or college was not "for them."[24]

The children of parents with higher education and income are also more likely to perform well academically. They are more at ease with the language, assumptions, and behaviour required of them at school. They are more likely to have books and, in recent years, Internet access at home. These too are factors that Bourdieu identifies as social or cultural capital. Higher-income families have more of the good old-fashioned money capital, too, which is a factor of increasing importance as governments cut back their support to education and as tuition fees rise at postsecondary institutions. University tuition fees rose by 86 per cent in real dollars, that is, after discounting for inflation, between 1983 and 1995 — a period in which average family incomes stagnated — and they have since continued to rise.[25] In 1997-98 they increased by another 9 per cent. Many universities have begun charging higher fees for professional programs. Fees for medicine, dentistry, engineering, and architecture are much higher than fees for basic undergraduate arts programs. In some cases the tuition fees are expected to cover the entire cost of the program. For example, the Executive MBA program at Queen's University cost $52,000 in 1997/98.[26] Nevertheless, university enrolment continued to increase in Canada up to the early 1990s despite a rapid decline in the population of eighteen- to twenty-four-year-olds, the group that makes up the majority of university students. After 1993, however, full-time university enrolment began to level off or decline marginally in most provinces, and part-time enrolment dropped sharply. This suggests that rising tuition fees may be an increasing barrier to access to postsecondary education for low-income students.

⋙⋘

The education system has not always been viewed as being so critical to employment chances in Canada. Before the Second World War, most employers did not look to the education system for skilled workers. Most youth did not complete high school before moving into occupations in the primary sector and manufacturing or, in the case of women, domestic roles. Apprenticeship as a system of training was limited to a small number of the skilled trades.[27] Immigration provided many of the skilled workers that employers needed.

This situation changed in the postwar period. The economic expansion in Canada in the twenty years following the war opened up a wide range of new skilled occupations. Employers still relied on immigration for skilled workers, but increasingly looked to the education system as well. Human capital theory emphasized the importance of education to economic growth. At the same time social critics like John Porter, in his book *The Vertical Mosaic*, were calling for broader access to education as a way of promoting equality of opportunity. These influences led to heavy investment in education systems by the federal and provincial governments by the 1960s.

Many other countries, especially the corporatist welfare states of continental Europe, drew a sharp distinction between the education system and institutions of occupational training. Employers, unions, and the state co-operated to provide young people with occupational skills. In Canada, as in the United States, with the liberal welfare state model, the education system was assigned the task of both academic and occupational training. Schools, colleges, and universities incorporated vocational programs into the curriculum, offering a wide variety of choices. Students approached this system as consumers; there was considerable

freedom to choose from the variety of programs offered, both at the secondary and postsecondary levels. Some call this the "cafeteria model" of
education. Students choose for themselves from among the range of programs offered. In doing so they stream themselves rather than being
streamed by school authorities. They assume responsibility for planning
their own educational careers based on their aspirations, abilities, and
knowledge of the labour market.[28]

This system has also been called the "market model" of
education.[29] It fits well with human capital theory, which assumes that
individuals invest in their own human capital growth on a rational basis,
with an eye to opportunities in the labour market, and then go out to
compete in that market with the skills and credentials acquired in the
education system. This is now the predominant view of education, particularly postsecondary education, in Canada and the United States. In
both countries the education system is relatively open. People who can
meet the academic entry requirements and pay whatever fees are
demanded can enter almost any program they want to, at any age. This
system gives students a great deal more choice than other models, but it
also places most of the risk on the individuals themselves. They must
choose wisely or be seen as the authors of their own misfortunes if their
credentials turn out to have little value in the labour market.

By contrast, the "institutional model" of education and training
practised in some countries creates a more structured set of relationships
between schools, employers, state agencies, and unions. In Japan, for
example, firms in the private sector form long-term relationships with
schools, assigning to schools a particular number of placements for graduates each year. The schools rank their students and nominate them to
the firms. Graduates placed in the firms then receive further occupational training from their employers. For students, academic performance is the critical factor; they strive to gain access to the best schools
and then to achieve the highest possible ranking there. The system
reduces the level of uncertainty, but offers little individual choice. Moreover, in times of recession it becomes more difficult for Japanese firms
to maintain their commitments to new hirings each year.

Germany provides another example of the institutional model.
There three-quarters of the youth enter apprenticeships or vocational
training when they leave secondary school. Apprentices train for three
or four years within a system that is run co-operatively by employers,
unions, and the state, combining practical experience and classroom
training. Apprentices receive a small training allowance from their
employers, eliminating the need for student loans or grants from the

state. The apprenticeship system is the only access route to a wide variety of occupations in Germany. The approach creates a highly defined occupational structure and carries the danger of some rigidity, but the Germans attempt to keep the system responsive to changing skill needs in the economy. Some four out of five apprentices who enter regular employment at the end of their terms do so with the firm they trained at. Despite this success rate, increasing numbers of German youth prefer to bypass the apprenticeship system and proceed to higher education at a university or technical college in the same way that North American youth do. Graduates of these institutions can expect to have higher lifetime earnings and greater career flexibility.[30]

The North American approach to education, then, appears to have some advantages over models that reduce the level of uncertainty about outcomes. It burdens the student with a greater degree of individual risk, but it provides more choice and is more forgiving of those who leave the system for a time and decide to return to it later. International organizations such as UNESCO (United Nations Educational, Scientific, and Cultural Organization) and the OECD (Organization for Economic Co-operation and Development) now advocate that education systems elsewhere adopt the openness and flexibility of North American education.[31]

Despite these strengths, the risks involved in the market model of education make the flaws in Canada's education systems, whether real or perceived, much more urgent concerns. As education has become more and more critical to the life chances of young people, it has moved to centre stage as a political issue.

><

Canadian education systems have come under fire from several directions in recent years. Debates range over several broad, interrelated areas. Many of the critics question the quality of education in Canadian elementary and secondary schools and point to Canada's mediocre rankings in comparative international tests as evidence.[32] Some criticize the structure and governance of education systems and complain of excessive bureaucratization, lack of accountability for results, inefficiency, and rising costs.[33] Business interests doubt the adequacy of the employability skills of recent graduates and raise the related issue of the role of education in promoting Canadian economic competitiveness.[34] Others, principally educators, condemn the retreat from liberal education and the excessive focus on preparation of youth for the labour market.[35] Student groups attack rising tuition costs as barriers to access to postsecondary education, while other social critics point out that schools continue to serve the purpose of slotting and streaming youth into the various strata of an increasingly unequal social structure.[36]

Dissatisfaction is widespread. A 1990 Canadian Education Association poll reported that only 6 per cent of Canadians would give the schools in their area an "A" (down from 19 per cent in 1979), while 45 per cent would give them a "C" or lower. Satisfaction was extremely low concerning the performance of schools in preparing students for working life.[37] This finding reflects a common perception that the quality of elementary and secondary education has declined since the 1960s. Many critics attribute this to the methods of progressive education such as those recommended by Ontario's 1968 Hall-Dennis Report, as well as the elimination of external, province-wide examinations, especially at the completion of high school. A related criticism is that high-school grades are inflated and that different standards apply at different schools even within the same school boards.

Those who defend the schools and teachers point out that the task of education is much more difficult now than it was a generation ago. The urban centres have large numbers of students who do not speak English or French as their first language. More students are staying in school, and there is downward pressure on education budgets. In 1994 Maude Barlow and Heather-jane Robertson launched a counterattack on the critics with their best-selling book *Class Warfare*. They maintained that a close examination of international test results shows that Canadian students have performed reasonably well and that the quality of education in Canadian schools is not as bad as the critics claim. They warned that criticisms of the quality of public education, combined with funding cutbacks, are a prelude to a much higher level of privatization of educational services and of higher corporate involvement in what remains of the public school system.[38]

Increasingly these debates are spilling out from books and newspapers onto the streets as governments of all stripes take action to respond to the demand for reform. The efforts of the Mike Harris Conservatives in Ontario to take control of education away from school boards and teachers and centralize it in the provincial government by legislation provoked a province-wide, two-week teachers' strike in the fall of 1997. Teachers in Alberta took job action in response to the reforms and cutbacks introduced there by the Conservative government led by Ralph Klein. Some provincial governments do seem to be pursuing elements of a Thatcherite strategy to introduce competition and private-sector involvement in the public school system. The evidence points to considerable private-sector interest in the education system — not only as a source of skilled workers but also as a market for curriculum materials and for direct provision of private schooling — as Barlow and Robertson claim. But to attribute the impetus for educational reform entirely to the corporate agenda misses the main point. The pressure for change comes primarily from anxious middle-class parents who see threats to their children's future livelihoods and standards of living in a more competitive and polarized labour market. They want to give their children every possible advantage in preparing to enter this economy. Their children need good grades to be admitted to universities and colleges, and they need them from good schools. The wealthy do not have this anxiety. They can send their children to private schools, knowing that over 95 per cent of the graduates there continue on to postsecondary institutions, most to the programs and universities of their choice.[39]

Middle-class parents must find ways to give their children advantages within the public system. They do this, when they can, by residing in the neighbourhoods that have the best public schools, by having their children placed in enriched streams for gifted students, and by hiring tutors.[40] Many also push for more choice, for example by pressuring governments to allow charter schools that operate like private schools but with public funding. Here their children can have a traditional education complete with school uniforms, rigorous systems of reward and punishment, and a strong emphasis on core subjects.[41] Some parents also vote for political parties that promise educational reform with a strong emphasis on a "back-to-basics" curriculum, a prominent feature in the platforms of right-wing populist parties like those of Harris and Klein. Activists on the left, concerned with protecting public education and the interests of teachers, are at risk of underestimating the depth of the anxiety felt by middle-class parents on this issue.

These debates are not limited to the subject of public school systems. Critics argue that the postsecondary level has also seen a decline in standards of quality. The drastic reductions in federal transfers to the provinces for postsecondary education that followed from the Liberal government's 1995 budget — the most severe in a long string of funding cutbacks — induced a period of turbulence and sweeping change in Canada's universities and colleges. Even before 1995, the gradual whittling away of funding for postsecondary education had resulted in reduced quality in such areas as student-faculty ratios, libraries, and laboratories.[42] The major cuts flowing from the 1995 federal budget prompted a radical rethinking of strategies at universities and colleges across the country. Tuition fees were climbing, and postsecondary institutions were taking a more entrepreneurial approach to the design and delivery of programs. Many universities now offer high-cost, accelerated programs geared to specific niches in the labour market — programs once considered to be the sole domain of community colleges. For example, for a fee of $10,750 the University of Calgary offers a nine-month certificate course in object-oriented software technology with guaranteed three-month minimum placements with such firms as Canadian Pacific Railway and TransCanada PipeLines. The program even offers prearranged loans from the Royal Bank to cover the full cost of tuition.[43] This kind of program, and its associated fees, can only be expected to increase in the years ahead.

The strategies available to institutions vary with their size, location, and prestige. The University of Toronto launched a $400 million fundraising campaign focused primarily on large, private-sector donors and aiming to amass a $1 billion endowment fund by the year 2000. Other Canadian universities have smaller-scale fundraising strategies, but these can only provide part of the solution to their problems. The large universities have advantages in competing for research funds, increasingly forming partnerships with the private sector. Smaller institutions seek to distinguish themselves in the education marketplace by transforming themselves into polytechnics, focusing on occupational training and specializing in their particular strengths. Meanwhile, downsizings attack the problem from the other side of the balance sheet.

No public leadership has been forthcoming from federal or provincial governments to deal with these issues. Universities, particularly, are being left to work out their own fates, although in Nova Scotia the provincial government has been actively pressuring the province's thirteen universities to merge large areas of their programs and administration. The scenario emerging for postsecondary education, according to some, is a tiered system similar to that in the United States. At the apex would be Canada's big three, "Ivy League North" — Toronto, University of British Columbia, and Queen's — holding the lion's share of research, fundraising dollars, and sought-after students and faculty members. Tuition fees and entrance requirements at those universities could rise to levels considerably higher than many of those in lower tiers. The remaining members of Canada's big ten — Alberta, Western, McMaster, Waterloo, McGill, Montreal, and Laval — would still be large institutions with programs across the broad range of disciplines, each attempting to use its strengths to advantage. Beneath this tier would come schools focused primarily on teaching undergraduates, some with specialized postgraduate programs and research in particular areas, comparable to state universities in the United States. The community college systems in each province would continue to offer programs geared to occupational training, as well as university entrance preparation in Quebec.[44]

Meanwhile, private training companies are sprouting up quickly in centres that have a high demand for workers with specialized skills. In Ottawa, for example, several companies offer intensive programs in information technology for people aiming to work in the region's high-tech sector. Fees can be as high as $16,000 for a twelve-month course, but bank loans are readily available. Private training companies also deliver a number of accelerated, high-fee programs offered by the local community college.

In 1998 the federal government announced a plan to switch a large portion of its support for postsecondary education away from transfers via the provinces towards direct transfers to students: the Millennium Fund, a $2.5 billion endowment to an arms-length scholarship-granting body established for an initial ten-year period scheduled to begin in the year 2000. This plan has the political advantage of placing the federal government directly in the role of benevolent uncle to Canada's youth. Knowing the popularity of such a fund, politicians are already jockeying for the credit. Prime Minister Jean Chrétien, it is said, wants it to be the centrepiece of his legacy upon leaving office, while Finance Minister Paul Martin manoeuvres to be seen as Canada's unofficial minister of education.[45] This is another approach that owes much to Margaret Thatcher. Providing resources directly to students makes them customers and consumers, promoting competition among the universities and colleges for their business. The impact of the approach on universities was quickly felt. Many began to develop advertising campaigns using standard marketing techniques to promote brand recognition of their names and to put forward their unique selling points.

Some degree of differentiation and competition among universities and colleges could be healthy, and earning a higher percentage of their revenue from tuition fees could make them more accountable to their students for the quality of education. The question is whether Canadian youth will have access to the kind of education and training they need to make their way in the economy and society they are entering. The concept of a scholarship fund of sufficient size to assist all who need it to pay rising tuition fees is positive in principle. It remains to be seen whether the Fund will be adequate to the purpose. And even if it is of a sufficient size, the chances are, based on the record so far, that it will not prove to be of benefit to low-income youth but will tend to be appropriated by the middle- and upper-class youth who have much better prospects of continuing on to postsecondary studies.

5 Making Their Way: The Labour-Market Experience

For most youth, entry to the labour market begins with a student job. The student labour market came into existence during the twentieth century as youth stayed in school longer and delayed their entry into full-time work. Students worked after school, on weekends, and during summer holidays, typically in jobs of the secondary labour market. During the 1970s and 1980s the student labour market grew rapidly in Canada, due both to the increased supply of student workers and the increased demand for them by employers.

The supply grew because of a combination of factors: the members of the baby-boom generation aged fifteen to twenty-four were still increasing in numbers until about 1980; young people were staying in school longer; and the percentage of female students entering the labour force increased. The demand grew because of new employer strategies. In the increasingly competitive economy, more employers wanted low-cost, just-in-time employees.

This lower end of the labour market was one of the main areas of growth during the 1980s. Employers, both large and small, took advantage of the increasing supply of low-cost labour by hiring students for a wide variety of part-time and temporary jobs, particularly in the consumer-service industries such as retail trade, food and beverage service,

accommodation, and tourism, in jobs such as sales clerks, cashiers, wait-
ers, and food-counter attendants. These were the McJobs, defined by
Douglas Coupland in his novel **Generation X** as "low-pay, low-prestige,
low-dignity, low-benefit, no-future jobs in the service sector. Frequently
considered a satisfying career choice by people who have never had
one."[1] Many of these dead-end jobs were not new. Previously they had
been performed by adult women or members of minority groups who
had difficulty getting access to jobs in the primary labour market.

In the 1980s, due partly to the increasing number of students, the
student labour market remained an important part of the economy
despite the shrinking size of the age group. A part-time job became common for students in their late teens and early twenties. Many of these
students continued to live at home, or even if they lived away from
home at university or college many continued to receive support from
their parents. Income from their student jobs supplemented the family
income. For many, especially teenagers living at home, their jobs were a
source of disposable income that gave them a degree of autonomy from
their parents. For others, wages from student jobs eased the pressure on
a family income that had to cover tuition fees and their living expenses.
In either case, the income tended to be invested in themselves; the custom by which youth were obliged to contribute to household income
had largely disappeared during the golden age for most members of
middle-income and higher-income families. The low wages, part-time
hours, and insecurity of student jobs were not major problems for them
because their jobs were not critical to meeting basic needs. But for students from low-income families, student jobs made an important contribution to the family income and helped to keep them in school.

Among students, a thin line exists between being unemployed and
dropping out of the labour market, especially during the school year.
The difference amounts to what a student says when responding to a
survey. If there are few job opportunities, students tend to report that
they are not looking for work. For this reason, the best indicator of
trends in the student labour market is not the unemployment rate,
which counts only those who are looking for work, but the employment
rate, the percentage of the total population with jobs. As the student
labour market grew from 1980 to 1989, the percentage of students who
held a job at any given time during the school year increased from 31 to
41 per cent. In the recession of the early 1990s the employment rate of
students dropped off sharply, and it continued to decline until 1996,
when it stood at 32 per cent. Most of this decline was experienced by
teenagers; the employment rate during the school year of students

aged twenty to twenty-four stayed at around 40 per cent through the 1990s.[2]

Students also had more difficulty finding summer jobs in the 1990s. Their employment rate fell from 69 per cent in July 1989 to 52 per cent in July 1996. Again, teenagers had the greatest difficulty of all finding work, but students in the twenty to twenty-four age group also had lower summer employment rates than that same group experienced in the late 1980s. Moreover, the percentage of summer jobs that were part-time increased from 48 per cent in 1989 to 58 per cent in 1996. Many student jobs have been held both during the school year and the summer, with an increase in the number of hours during the summer, but recently the trend has been towards student jobs remaining part-time during the summer. This has been especially true of restaurant jobs, where only one-quarter of student summer jobs were full-time by 1997.[3]

We tend not to worry much about students who can't find jobs. Our stereotype is the teenager who earns a wage at McDonald's and spends it at The Gap, or vice-versa. The trend towards withdrawing from the labour market and staying in school longer may be viewed as positive, but since 1989 the percentage of fifteen- to twenty-four-year-olds with no work experience has doubled, moving from 10 to 20 per cent.[4] Student wages are also becoming more critical. As tuition levels increase for postsecondary studies, the household incomes of middle-class families have stagnated or declined. As a result student jobs become more important as a source of revenue to cover education costs. Declining student jobs, stagnant family incomes, and rising tuition costs will combine to increase the financial pressures on students and their families, especially families whose incomes are in decline.

Some parents worry that a job during the school year interferes with a student's academic performance and could even lead to dropping out. Indeed, a job opportunity can be one factor in a decision to drop out of high school, but research shows that parents should not worry about their children having jobs requiring a moderate number of hours per week. The lowest dropout rates occur among students who have part-time jobs — that is, jobs of up to twenty hours per week. Those who work more than twenty hours per week, and those who have no jobs at all, are much more likely to drop out. Among young women, having no job at all is an even greater risk factor than working more than twenty hours per week. This pattern occurs regardless of other risk factors, which suggests that a part-time student job brings with it an added benefit. It is not clear whether this benefit comes because having a job increases a student's self-esteem and work ethic or if it reflects the prior existence of these traits. It could be that work experience in mini-mum-wage jobs helps to convince students that completing high school is critical if they hope to do better as adults.[5]

Student jobs are an important feature of the North American econ-omy and culture. They provide students with income and give employ-ers access to a low-cost labour force for a wide variety of occupations. But when they finish school and go out looking for a "career" job, young people expect more. Here they encounter several problems.

><><

The first problem is unemployment. High youth unemployment is some-times played down as an issue, because after all, it is said, youth don't really need the income when most of them are still living at home and going to school. But the unemployment rate of students is much lower than the average rate for all youth, in part because students withdraw from the labour market when they cannot find jobs. Young people who are no longer attending school part-time or full-time have much higher rates of unemployment than students.

Most young men and women enter the labour market when they leave school. But entering the labour market, in the official parlance, does not necessarily mean that they have a job. It means they are either working or actively looking for work. To be counted as unemployed, a person must be actively looking for work. We sometimes hear that large numbers of young people have disappeared into the ranks of the "hid-den unemployed," where they have become "discouraged workers." When Statistics Canada researchers looked into this question they found that the percentage of youth aged fifteen to twenty-four who were nei-ther in school nor in the labour market — that is, not even looking for work — had been declining gradually and by the mid-1990s stood at about 6 per cent of the age group. But of this 6 per cent of youth, less than one in ten could have been described as discouraged. Half of them were young mothers with child-care responsibilities — most of them liv-ing with their spouses, a third living as single parents, and the rest living with their parents or other relatives. Most of these young mothers had not completed high school. The other half of the 6 per cent were equally divided between women and men and were, again, primarily early school leavers. Their reasons for not looking for work varied: some had other personal responsibilities, some were suffering from illness, and some were about to start a new job at the time of the survey and were therefore not looking for another. Less than 0.4 per cent of the total age group were classed as "discouraged workers" — people who had given up looking for work because they thought no work was available or because they simply did not want to work.[6]

In other words, young people do not seem to have lost the work ethic. Nevertheless, the transition from school to work became more difficult in the 1990s, and the picture late in the decade had not improved significantly despite a general economic recovery. Non-student youth in the fifteen to twenty-four age group had an unemployment rate of 15 per cent in 1990. The rate rose to 20 per cent in 1992, then dropped back a little, but remained at 18 per cent in 1996, despite the economic recovery and declining unemployment rates for older workers.[7] Because there is considerable flux in and out of employment, the percentage of non-student youth who have experienced unemployment is much higher than this. Unemployment is a common experience during the school-work transition. Even among youth leaving school with postsecondary qualifications, close to half go through periods of unemployment in the two years following graduation.[8]

Even so, young workers with postsecondary credentials are much better off than those without. There is a strong relationship between education levels and unemployment rates. In 1996, when the average unemployment rate of non-student youth aged fifteen to twenty-four was 18 per cent, the rate for those with only "some high school" but no diploma was 28 per cent, while the rates were much lower for high-school graduates (16 per cent), those with trade certificates (16 per cent), community college graduates (12 per cent), and university graduates (10 per cent).[9] Moreover, the unemployment rates of university and college graduates decline over the five years after they leave school until they are well below the average rate for all age groups. For example, the unemployment rate of Canada's university graduating class of 1990 was 11 per cent in 1992 and 6 per cent in 1995; for college graduates of 1990, the rates were 10 per cent in 1992 and 7 per cent in 1995. (The national unemployment rates for all age groups in 1992 and 1995 were 11.3 per cent and 9.5 per cent respectively.)[10]

Both college and university graduates show significant differences in unemployment rates by field of study. Graduates in the health sciences, both university and college, tended to do best in the 1990s, although the retrenchment in health services that followed from the federal government's 1995 budget may have worked to change their prospects. University graduates in the humanities, fine and applied arts, agriculture, and biological sciences all tend to have unemployment rates above the average for their total graduating class, while those in engineering, social sciences, mathematics, and the physical sciences all have about average rates. College graduates in the arts have unemployment rates that are above average, while all others are close to average.[11] But even those with the worst prospects among university and college graduates — those in fine and applied arts — still have unemployment rates that are lower than the average of those youth who have only a secondary school diploma or less.

Young women aged twenty-two to twenty-four who had left school without a high-school diploma had an unemployment rate of over 30 per cent in 1995.[12] Women find it difficult to enter many of the occupations open to young male leavers — blue-collar jobs in construction, forestry, and mining, for example. Many young women without high-school diplomas withdraw from the labour market completely, so that their employment rate is less than 50 per cent. At higher levels of education, the male and female employment rates converge.

Young people who have aboriginal status, who are members of visible minorities, or who have disabilities have higher rates of unemployment than others with the same educational qualifications. For example, in 1992 the unemployment rate for 1990 community colleges graduates who were not members of these groups was 10 per cent, but for aboriginal graduates of the same programs the unemployment rate was 18 per cent, for visible minorities 15 per cent, and for the disabled 14 per cent.[13] Regionally, across Canada the unemployment rate of non-students aged fifteen to twenty-four varied in 1996 from a high of 38 per cent in Newfoundland to a low of 11 per cent in Alberta. The rate was over 20 per cent everywhere east of the Ottawa River, about average in Ontario and British Columbia, and well under average in the Prairie provinces.[14]

High youth unemployment reflects a weak demand in the labour market for young workers. But another source of the problem is the weak links between the education system and employers, which means that even well-educated youth are required to spend a period of time unemployed while they search for work. Many young people don't have any clear idea about how to find a job. The quality of career counselling is uneven across Canada and unavailable to many young people who need it. The counselling services of a Human Resources Centre are usually limited to those receiving employment insurance. Programs offered by community-based agencies are often targeted to particular groups, such as welfare recipients. Young workers who have left school and are not eligible for employment insurance may have no access to career counselling of any kind apart from expensive private services.[15]

Some countries have well-established links between school and work, as we've seen in the case of Germany's apprenticeship system, where most youth move from the education system directly into a program of occupational training, much of which takes place in a real workplace (see chapter 4).[16] The system does not guarantee that there will be jobs in the adult labour market, but it does reduce the time lost in looking for work. As a result, the youth unemployment rates in countries with this kind of system stay much closer to the rate for all age groups. Such bridges between school and work are lacking in Canada, as they are in the United States, and building them has become the focus of many of the youth employment programs introduced in North America in the last ten years. Co-op education, internships, "work experience" programs, youth apprenticeships, and expanded information and counselling services — all are designed to create better links between school and work.

><

When they do find work, young Canadians move into labour-market segments that are strongly determined by their education levels and gender. It quickly becomes clear that "the labour market" is an abstraction that holds multiple realities.[17]

Let's look first at those who leave school without completing a high-school diploma. At this level of education the labour markets for men and women are different worlds. Most of the employed men in this group work in blue-collar jobs, primarily in construction, manufacturing, and the primary sector. About one-quarter of these young men work as skilled tradesmen by the time they reach the age of twenty-four. Typical occupations are carpenter, welder, heavy duty mechanic, and auto mechanic. They learn their skills and earn credentials in various ways, including practical experience, apprenticeship, and formal study at a trade or vocational school or college, despite their lack of a high-school diploma. Others, about one in fifteen, rise to supervisory sales or service positions by the age of twenty-four. But the majority of employed young men without high-school diplomas work in semi-skilled and unskilled blue-collar, sales, and service jobs, such as delivery drivers, grocery clerks, kitchen helpers, and general labourers — jobs that in many cases are distinguished from the student labour market, if at all, only by the number of hours worked per week.

Less than half of the young women without a high-school diploma have jobs at all. In 1995 the majority were either unemployed or had withdrawn from the labour market. Of those who have jobs, about two-thirds work in sales and service occupations in the consumer-service industries, for example as retail sales clerks, cashiers, and waitresses. A smaller number, about 14 per cent, work in blue-collar occupations — primarily skilled and semi-skilled jobs, such as seamstresses and food-processing machine operators — of a type held by few if any males.

This pattern of gender-divided labour markets also holds true for those who complete a high-school diploma but have not completed a postsecondary degree, diploma, or certificate. Over 70 per cent of these female high-school graduates work in clerical, sales, and service occupations, primarily in consumer-service industries. Large numbers of the men also work in clerical, sales, and service occupations, but about half work in blue-collar jobs, compared to less than 10 per cent of the women. Close to half of the male high-school graduates work in jobs that do not require a high-school diploma — jobs such as truck drivers, security guards, grocery clerks, and service station attendants. Many of these young high-school graduates could be said to be stuck in the student labour market.

Very different patterns of employment appear among young workers who leave the education system with a postsecondary degree, diploma, or certificate. By the age of twenty-four about half of the university graduates, both male and female, work in professional or managerial occupations, and another 13 or 14 per cent work in skilled technical occupations below the professional level. Here, too, there are distinct gender patterns. Men with university degrees are much more likely than women to work in professional jobs in the natural and applied sciences, including engineering, as well as in business, finance, and administration. Female university graduates are more likely to be teachers, especially in elementary and secondary schools. But among young university graduates aged twenty-four or under, over a third of both sexes still work in clerical, sales, service, or blue-collar occupations typical of the student labour market. This is another aspect of the school-work transition difficulties of young university graduates. In the early years after graduation, not only do they pass through periods of unemployment, but large numbers of them also continue to work in what is considered to be the student labour market while looking for career jobs.

Among those who complete a diploma or certificate at a community college or other non-university institution, over one-third of the men work in blue-collar jobs, primarily in skilled trades. Another one-third of the men have skilled technical jobs, especially in natural and applied sciences. Over half of the women work in professional, manage-
ial and technical occupations, particularly in nursing, teaching, and administrative and business occupations. Almost a third of the

male and close to half of the female college graduates, however, are still working in semi-skilled and unskilled clerical, sales, and service occupations by the age of twenty-four, once again reflecting the difficulties of finding career jobs.

The age of twenty-four is still early days for university and college graduates. How does this picture change over time? If we look again to the class of 1990 — those who had full-time jobs only — by 1995, five years after graduation, about 17 per cent of those with a bachelor's degree were working in jobs that required no postsecondary qualifications. Among those with master's degrees, only 6 per cent worked in jobs that required no postsecondary qualifications. Of those who received a doctorate in 1990, the number working at jobs requiring less than a university degree was negligible. Contrary to popular myth, legions of Ph.D.s are not out there driving taxis. Of 1990's community college graduates, however, five years after graduation over a third had jobs that required no postsecondary qualifications.[18]

Underemployment of this kind may be a serious long-term problem for a significant minority of youth who graduated from a university or college in the 1990s. In the labour force as a whole, one employed person in four is already underemployed in a current job.[19] A clear pattern is emerging. Those with low levels of education have high rates of unemployment. Large numbers of those with high-school diplomas and postsecondary degrees, diplomas, and certificates are working in jobs that do not require their qualifications, even five years after graduation. The pattern is one of downward displacement — people with postsecondary credentials squeezing out those with only a high-school diploma; those with high-school diplomas displacing early leavers. This may be the outcome of the disjuncture between the high aspirations of youth and the actual opportunities in the labour market.

Part of the problem may be the result of a poor information flow between the education system and the labour market. Unemployment and underemployment are higher for graduates in certain fields of study, particularly the arts and humanities. In the past few years we have also heard reports of problems for graduates in certain professional fields, including law, accounting, dentistry, economics, and some branches of engineering. At the same time, the rapid growth of high-tech industries has left employers with shortages of skilled labour in a number of applied science fields, especially computer engineering. We know that most students enter postsecondary education with career objectives in mind. In some cases the problem may arise from the lack of good labour-market information and career counselling.

Another type of underemployment is involuntary part-time employ-ment. Statistics Canada defines a part-time job as anything less than thirty hours per week. In the twenty years from 1976 to 1996, the inci-dence of part-time jobs held by youth aged fifteen to twenty-four increased from 21 per cent to 45 per cent. Much of this increase is because youth are staying in school longer; 90 per cent of student jobs are part-time.[20] If we look only at non-students in the age group of twenty-two to twenty-four, the picture is different. Here we find that 10 per cent of the employed men and 21 per cent of the employed women were working part-time in 1995.[21] Of these, a little less than half of both groups were doing so involuntarily. In other words, among non-student youth in this age group, women experience roughly twice as much involuntary part-time employment as men. The total incidence is not high, but when it is added to the unemployment rates and the num-bers of youth working in jobs for which they are overqualified, we begin to get a more complete picture of the degree of underemployment of this generation's skills and energy.

Other forms of non-standard employment include temporary jobs, self-employment, and holding multiple jobs. The incidence of temporary jobs has been increasing, especially among young postsecondary gradu-ates, where they account for over 20 per cent of all jobs.[22] Since the 1980s the percentage of jobs that last six months or less has grown, while the percentage of those lasting between six months and five years has declined.[23] This growth of temporary jobs is an indicator of the increased contingency and insecurity in today's labour market. The phe-nomenon has an impact on workers of all ages, and young workers may be more likely to see it as normal. They assume that employers have a limited commitment to them, and they in turn have a limited commit-ment to their employers. In the United States, where this trend is well advanced, the attitude is called "Free Agent USA" and symbolized by the line from the film *Jerry Maguire*: "Show me the money." Workers are encouraged to view themselves as "companies of one" and their employers as their customers or clients.[24] They are encouraged not to expect any more loyalty from an employer than they would expect from a customer and to view every job as an opportunity to enhance their skills and resumés for the next job. Loyalty and commitment decline on both sides. In certain professional occupations, this may not be an issue. Employers may view knowledge workers as they do other professionals, like lawyers and accountants, who have a long tradition of indepen-dence from their clients, and this attitude may be advantageous to those whose skills are in demand. But for workers in less-skilled jobs, the growing contingency means less job security, few if any benefits, and no opportunities for advancement within a company.

Self-employment accounts for less than 10 per cent of the employment of young Canadians aged twenty-two to twenty-four. Its incidence is highest among men without postsecondary qualifications, where it is concentrated in certain blue-collar occupations, such as truck drivers, chainsaw and skidder operators, and craftsmen. Among males with postsecondary qualifications, self-employment is spread across professional and technical occupations, such as financial analysts and computer programmers, skilled trades, and retail and wholesale sales occupations. Among young women, self-employment is also highest among those without postsecondary education, typically in sales and service occupations such as hairstylists, food-counter servers, and cashiers. Among women with postsecondary qualifications, over half of self-employment is in the retail trade.[25]

Many young workers hold more than one job as they attempt to assemble a full-time income from the work opportunities available in the economy. But the group with the highest rate of multiple job-holding is women with postsecondary qualifications. Again looking at the non-students aged twenty-two to twenty-four, about 19 per cent of female university graduates held multiple jobs in 1995, compared to 14 per cent of the males. Most of these university-educated women still had their main job in the student labour market, typically working as sales clerks or cashiers. Only one in five had her main job at the managerial, professional, or technical levels. The picture was quite different for male university graduates with multiple jobs. About four in five of them had their main jobs at the managerial, professional, or technical levels.

Among those with a community college diploma or certificate, women were also much more likely to have multiple jobs, but gender disparity was not so evident in the type of job. About half of both men and women had their main jobs at the managerial, professional, or technical levels. Many of the women had their main jobs in health-related occupations, such as nursing, while the men tended to have their main jobs in one of the skilled trades. Of those without postsecondary education, the gender pattern was similar. Women were more likely to hold multiple jobs than men.[26]

><><

Unemployment, underemployment, insecure employment — all are common experiences of youth in the Canadian labour market. So too are low earnings. But the quality of work itself is another element in the labour-market experience. What is it like to work in the jobs that young people are finding?

When young people themselves are asked, they report that the best jobs are the professional, managerial, and technical occupations available to the more fortunate graduates of universities and colleges. Those jobs have better pay and benefits and more opportunities for advancement, and employees can use their skills and knowledge in fields related to their education. The broader public sector — health, education, and the public service — used to be a major employer of new graduates in these categories, but most new jobs are now in the private sector. Management consulting firms, law offices, engineering companies, banks and brokerages, advertising agencies, and high-tech manufacturers are the typical employers now. It is possible to earn a good salary in many of these workplaces, but the working conditions are stressful. The twelve-hour working day is not uncommon, and members of the junior professional staff have little choice but to meet such demands. Sociologist John Hagan, in his study of the legal profession in Toronto, has called these exploited young workers the "professional proletariat."[27] There is often a fiercely competitive environment and a macho work ethic. These values are reinforced in the popular media, for example in the television program *Traders*, and increasingly in the pages of women's magazines. (We can be thankful, at least, for the satirical comic strip *Dilbert* for lampooning these values and the management strategies that support them.)

Much of the work in blue-collar occupations is also rated positively. Some skilled trades have a healthy number of job opportunities, especially when the economy is on an upswing, and they pay well. This labour-market segment is still heavily male-dominated, however, and subject to fluctuations in demand. Semi-skilled blue-collar occupations have been one of the main locations of job loss over the past two decades. There was a spurt of growth in blue-collar manufacturing jobs through the mid-1990s, led by the boom in exports, but this was not expected to last.

The take-up sector, and the place where work is least prized, is made up of clerical, sales, and service occupations, particularly in consumer-service industries. Here, young people report that the pay is low, the benefits poor or non-existent, and the chances for promotion slim at best. There are some managerial jobs — sales supervisors, shift managers, and the like — but the pay and working conditions are not much better than for regular workers. Many young workers say that they have little choice in their hours of work, have no freedom to make decisions, and are often required to follow rigid work procedures.[28]

Think of telemarketers, that army of young workers who seem ready to attack you by phone every evening at dinner time. They are just the most evident part of the growing labour force of teleworkers providing a wide range of services over the telephone lines. In her book *Whose Brave New World?* Heather Menzies describes the typical working conditions of teleworkers — low pay, few benefits, no job security, and no opportunity for personal development. The job is defined down to the last detail, and computers closely monitor work performance. Much of the work is evaluated in quantitative terms — the number of calls made or received per hour — whether the task is to sell financial services, handle insurance claims, or make hotel reservations. Youth are not the only workers in these occupations, but this is one of the growth areas of the economy, the destination for large numbers of new entrants to the labour market who cannot find career jobs.[29]

The organization and control of work in service jobs now are different from that experienced by workers a generation earlier. The growth of the service sector has demanded new thinking by management on methods of controlling and supervising the labour process to ensure efficiency and quality. In the old industrial model developed for the mass production of goods, the aim of scientific management was to break down the production process into discrete operations that could be measured and controlled to ensure that finished products were produced efficiently and met quality standards. In service jobs, the work to be supervised is not the production of a good but the provision of a service that is assessed by the level of customer satisfaction. The customer enters directly into the work process, making it difficult or impossible to control the behaviour of the worker by the old methods of scientific management.

New methods of controlling the labour process in service work fall into two broad categories — the production-line and empowerment approaches.[30] The production line is the direct extension of the old methods of scientific management into service work. A standard approach is to program work methods into computers to ensure that all operations can be performed in only one way. Telemarketers may be given predetermined scripts and prompted by their computer through each step of their pitch. Food-counter staff may be given routine lines to deliver or even songs to sing. Workers at Licks Burger & Ice Cream Shops, for example, sing jingles as they serve up the fast food. The aim is to take any autonomy or spontaneity out of the production process to ensure that it is delivered in precisely the way desired by management. Since the presence of supervisors would interfere with the worker-customer relationship, surveillance is indirect, by computer, video camera, customer comment cards, and the like. The production-line approach continues the tradition of deskilling work in much the same way as carried out on the assembly line.

The empowerment approach gives workers the chance to make decisions and to use their own judgement. This allows a more spontaneous interaction between worker and customer, enhancing the value of the service by including a personal relationship. Workers themselves become part of the product being offered to the customer. In the words of the president of Red Lobster USA, "The goal is to remove the spiel and inject the personality . . . to bring it down to an intensely personal experience."[31] Workers are prepared through careful selection and training to ensure that they develop the desired approach. The system may employ different methods of motivation, from standard sales commissions to the promotion of intense competition between employees.

In *The Managed Heart*, her study of flight attendants in the United States, Arnie Hochschild coined the expression "emotional labour" to describe service work that demands the display of states of feeling by the worker and the inducement of emotional responses in the customer. For some companies, this emotional exchange provides the key competitive edge in its industry, as reflected by slogans such as "At Speedy, you're a somebody." Hochschild points out that the demand on flight attendants to perform with the proper emotions leads to a form of method acting. The worker must not only display emotion but also do so with convincing sincerity by persuading herself of the authenticity of her feelings. Her company sells this emotion with the jingle, "Our smiles aren't just painted on." The result, Hochschild reports, is frequently burnout and an emotional numbness that the worker carries with her into her personal life.

The empowerment approach is used in both the upper levels of the service sector, including professional and technical occupations, and the lower levels, in areas such as direct sales and personal services. The production-line approach is used only in the bottom layer of service jobs, where most workers tend to be young, female, or members of minority groups who face discrimination in the labour market. Both approaches raise issues of basic respect for human dignity in the labour process. The precept that the customer is always right makes for an unequal relationship in the delivery of the service. The worker is expected to absorb the disrespect of customers. When this aspect of the job is combined with disrespect from the employer — as demonstrated by arbitrary behaviour, insufficient and irregular hours of work, low pay, and job insecurity — the employee can become intensely dissatisfied with the work situation. This experience has contributed to high rates of turnover in many McJobs of the consumer-service industries. Recently, however, after realizing that these are the only jobs available, many young workers have sought union protection as a strategy for improving their pay, status, and working conditions.

But very few young workers have unionized jobs. Only 11 per cent of employed workers aged fifteen to twenty-four were union members at the latest count, compared to 32 per cent of those aged twenty-five to forty-four, and 44 per cent of those aged forty-five to fifty-four.[32] These numbers reflect the greying of the labour movement. The highest rates of unionization are in the broader public sector and the blue-collar occupations, both of which have declining employment opportunities. Most new job creation in Canada is happening in the service sector, particularly in small firms, which are less likely not only to be unionized but also to offer much in the way of benefits. They are more likely to pay lower wages and lay off their workers.[33] Unionization offers its members many benefits, and the labour movement has played a historic role in improving the wages and working conditions of Canadians in the twentieth century, but today, by protecting the jobs of prime-age workers in the core jobs of the primary labour market, and by making seniority the principle to govern decisions on layoffs, unions are more likely to appear to young workers as barriers to their access to good jobs.

During the past few years a number of high-profile organizing drives have taken place in workplaces in which young people predominate: McDonald's in Orangeville, Ontario, St. Hubert, Quebec, and Squamish, B.C., several franchises of Starbucks Coffee, Casino Windsor, women's clothing shops Limité and Suzy Shier in Toronto, Wal-Mart in Windsor, and security guards at several firms in Ontario. Young workers have been prominent among the leadership, and some campaigns have been successful. Other attempts have led to the closing of the franchise and the layoff of its workers, a tactic that chains adopt to discourage organizing elsewhere. Some of Canada's major unions, including the Teamsters, the Canadian Auto Workers, the Steelworkers, the United Food and Commercial Workers, and the Union of Needletrades, Industrial, and Textile Employees (UNITE), have backed these organizing drives, and a certain momentum seems to be building. The conventional wisdom until recently has been that too many barriers stand in the way of organizing low-wage, service-sector workplaces in which women and young people make up the majority of employees. The workers were said to be too transient, apathetic, or intimidated by their employers. For their part, the unions did not appear interested in investing the large sums required in organizing drives for workers whose dues would never cover the costs of representing them. Now a major organizing battle seems to be shaping up, with young workers at the centre of it.[34]

✕

Employers and business-oriented research bodies like the Conference Board of Canada maintain that youth are not leaving school with adequate employability skills for today's workplaces. This may be true in a narrow band of technical and professional areas, but the larger picture appears to show the contrary: there are many well-educated youth and not enough jobs that make use of the skills they have to offer. One of the chief complaints of young workers in low-level service jobs is that they do not have the opportunity to display the skills acquired in the education system and elsewhere. A recent study found that 21 per cent of the people in Canada's employed workforce have jobs that do not make use of their literacy skills. For women and youth, the percentage is even higher. Only 5 per cent of the workforce, by contrast, needed literacy upgrading to handle the demands of their jobs. The researchers pointed out that people working in these jobs may not retain the level of skills they bring to them, that they are in danger of suffering skills loss over time. This possibility is masked by how skills are given credentials in our society. No one is going to take away your high-school diploma or university degree when you have been working in an unskilled job, but there is, nevertheless, a serious danger of "human capital depletion" arising from the loss of skills by workers who do not have access to jobs that utilize their skills. This state of affairs represents a potential loss both to the young workers themselves and to the society that has provided their education.[35]

The federal government, through Human Resources Development Canada (HDRC), continues to project growth in jobs that require a postsecondary qualification and a decline in semi-skilled and unskilled jobs. This, it says, is the long-term trend. Some employers in high-tech manufacturing have indeed expressed concerns about shortages of skilled workers in computer science, electrical engineering, and related fields. But in the short and medium terms the prospects for young workers appear to be quite different. HRDC expected to see a rapid decline in youth unemployment in the late 1990s, but even if this did occur a substantial share of the job growth for youth was expected to be in low-skill jobs. The highest levels of growth would be in the consumer-service industries: retail trade, accommodation and food, amusement and recreation, and personal and household services — all of which are prime locations for low-paying, low-skill, non-unionized jobs.[36] Some 54 per cent of all jobs created over the 1996-2000 period would require education or training equivalent to high school or less.[37] But 85 per cent of young Canadians now complete high school, and close to three-quarters of all youth undertake postsecondary education towards a degree, diploma, or certificate.[38]

The demand for skilled workers will continue to grow, but so too will the demand for workers to fill low-skill jobs. This prospect led one senior federal official to exclaim, "What we need are more illiterates!" But the supply of illiterates is falling. Young Canadians are responding to the call to stay in school and aspiring to rewarding careers in skilled occupations. The risk is that Canada, and the youth themselves, will lose the investment they have made in their future.

6 Changing Patterns: Earnings, Incomes, and Personal Life

D erek Holt, an economist with the Royal Bank, projects rosy financial prospects for today's generation of youth. Young people, he says, stand to receive large inheritances from their parents. He estimates that the 6.3 million parents of Canada's baby-boom generation will leave their money to the 9.8 million boomers born between 1947 and 1966. Then, in the next wave, these 9.8 million will leave their assets to only 7.3 million of their children born since 1980. "Simple math," he concludes, "suggests that young people will be better positioned through less splitting of wealth to benefit from inheritance activity than their boomer parents will be."[1]

But although prosperity may be just around the corner for those with rich parents, and those whose families have the means to support them now while they continue their education, it may still be far out of reach for most of those who are young now. A close analysis of the current and projected earnings of young workers in the labour market provides a more sobering account: not a golden future for all, but, more likely, increased social inequality.

A thicket of studies on earnings in Canada shows that young workers as a whole, men and women together, have been losing ground relative to older workers. The earnings of young Canadian workers appear to be following four major trends. First, the average earnings of young men have declined sharply since 1980, both in absolute terms and relative to men in older age groups. Second, the average earnings of young women have not declined to the same degree, either in absolute terms or relative to women in older age groups, and by some accounts they are improving. Third, although the gap between the earnings of young men and young women has narrowed, this has been due more to the decline of young men's earnings than to any increase in young women's earnings. And fourth, while the gap has widened between the earnings of young women with university degrees and those without postsecondary education, the discrepancy between the earnings of young male Canadian workers with different levels of education has remained about the same.

The topic of earnings has attracted a lot of attention in recent years because of concern about the declining middle class and social polarization in Canada. Leaving the question of age aside, the general trends indicate that although polarization has not increased in Canada, inequality has. That is, there has been no significant increase in the percentage of people making extremely high or extremely low earnings; the middle class is about the same size as it was in 1970. But there is greater inequality in earnings: workers in the low-income and middle-income categories are earning less, while those at the upper level are earning more. This increasing inequality in earnings has been offset to some degree by tax rates and social transfers, so that there has been less growth in the inequality of total incomes than of earnings from employment.[2]

A variety of metaphors have been used to explain the social structures of different periods. In the early industrial period, the social structure was pyramid-shaped, with a few wealthy people at the top and increasingly large numbers of the population as you move down the levels to the bottom. During the age of postwar prosperity, the social structure was said to be like a portly gentleman, with a large bulge in the middle. Advocates of the "disappearing middle" thesis in the 1980s said we were developing an "hourglass society," with large bulges polarized at the top and bottom. But we now seem to be moving towards something more pear-shaped — the portly gentleman's belly "goin' south."[3]

Between 1981 and 1993 the real annual earnings of men in the seventeen to twenty-four age group who were working full-year and full-time declined by about 15 per cent. Most of this loss happened during the recession of the early 1980s, but it was never regained in the period of recovery of the late 1980s, and their earnings declined again in the recession of the early 1990s. Men in the twenty-five to thirty-four age group also saw their earnings decline during this period, by about 7 per cent, and so too did men in the thirty-five to forty-four age group, while men in the older age groups experienced rising earnings. Young women working full-year and full-time also suffered falling real earnings in the early 1980s, but since that time the pattern has been reversed. The average earnings of all female age groups working full-year and full-time have been on the increase since about 1985.[4]

Keep in mind that an individual ages from one group to the next over time. The individuals aged seventeen to twenty-four in 1980 became thirty-five to forty-two in 1998. In this light, sharp differences in income between age groups may not be such a concern. If young men can look forward to a steep increase in their earnings over their lifetimes, perhaps they do not have anything to worry about. When they reach their forties and fifties they will be able to tell stories of their youthful poverty over vintage wines.

What matter more are not differences between age groups but differences between generations. Only time will tell for certain whether the current generation of youth will have incomes equal to or greater than their parents, but recent evidence is not encouraging. A 1997 study by researchers Paul Beaudry and David Green reveals a consistent pattern among male univesity graduates.[5] Over the last thirty years, each successive group of twenty-five- and twenty-six-year-olds — called a cohort — has average earnings that are considerably less than the previous cohorts at the same age. For example, those aged thirty-two in 1993 earned about 20 per cent less than those aged thirty-two in 1971, even after adjusting for differences in the business cycle. Moreover, the rate at which earnings increase with age declined with each successive cohort.

Among men with a high-school education or less, the pattern is slightly different. Each successive cohort from 1964 to 1978 had higher weekly earnings at the outset (age twenty-five to twenty-six) than its predecessors, but experienced declining wage growth as its members aged; then, for each successive cohort after 1978, earnings at the outset also declined, and as members aged they never reached the level of previous cohorts at the same age. There is a 20 per cent decline in average earnings from the 1978 cohort to the 1990 cohort at the same age.

Among women the findings for cohorts reflect what we have already seen for female age groups: no significant differences. Women with a high-school diploma or less all earn about the same amount across all cohorts and experience very little increase in earnings as they age. Their earnings are well below the averages for men in the same education group, but the gender earnings gap narrows for the younger cohorts because of the lower earnings of their male counterparts.

The female university-educated cohorts show a different pattern. The two earliest cohorts, those who were twenty-five to twenty-six in 1964 and 1968, had declining average earnings from their late twenties to their mid-thirties and rising earnings thereafter. Subsequent cohorts did not experience this dip. Apart from this, there is very little difference in average earnings among the cohorts at the same ages. Such difference as there is amounts to this: younger cohorts of women have lower earnings at the outset but more rapid increases as they age. When this pattern is projected into the future, university-educated women in younger cohorts would be expected, on average, to earn much more than their female predecessors by the time they are in their forties and fifties. The consequence is that the gender earnings gap for those with a university education, present and projected, is smaller with each successive cohort.

What workers who are young today will earn when they are fifty-four cannot be deduced by using algebra, but these are the trends, and if they continue the current generation of young males can expect to have much lower lifetime earnings for their level of education than the generation that preceded them. Young women with a high-school diploma or less can expect to have earnings that start out low and stay low, while women with a university education can, on average, expect to catch up to and even surpass their male counterparts by the time they are middle-aged. Beaudry and Green projected much higher earnings for university-educated young women by their forties on the basis of rapid gains in their late twenties and early thirties; they did not take into account the possibility that other contingencies, particularly motherhood, might interfere with these gains at a later age than for the preceding generation.[6]

><><

By the late 1990s there was still no consensus on the question of what causes these trends in the earnings patterns of young Canadian workers, though theories abounded. One theory is that a changing economy will reward those with greater experience. This would fit well with human capital theory, which holds that earnings increase with skills acquired through education and experience. Since younger workers tend to be better educated on average than older workers, the argument goes, the explanation for their deteriorating relative and absolute incomes must be related to the additional skills that older workers have acquired through experience. Steven Davis, a U.S. researcher, advanced this argument when he found that a growing gap between the earnings of younger and older workers occurred in every industrial country except Sweden during the 1980s. He speculated that it must be due to some common pattern of technological change or industrial restructuring that favoured workers with skills acquired through work experience.[7]

That theory does not stand up against the evidence. In Canada younger men earn less than earlier cohorts did with equivalent years of experience. This has been a consistent pattern over seven cohorts from 1964 to 1990, which suggests that something other than experience-based skill accounts for the difference. Skill based on formal education does not appear to be a major factor either, because the ratio of earnings of male university graduates relative to high-school graduates has not changed much in Canada,[8] while the inequality of younger and older workers with equivalent years of education has increased. It is possible that to some extent recent changes in demand in the economy — especially the introduction of new technology — favour workers with more years of experience, but this does not appear to be the only, or even the main, factor.

Another possible explanation is that industrial restructuring has altered the nature of job opportunities, especially for young men. This seems like an obvious candidate when we think of the decline of unionized blue-collar jobs, such as those held by autoworkers, paying over $20 an hour, compared to the growing number of McJobs in the consumer-service industries that pay barely above the minimum wage. But analysis of earnings patterns shows that the decline of young workers' earnings relative to older workers has occurred regardless of industry, occupation, education level, or union status.[9] It seems to be happening right across the labour market. A young worker in a manufacturing job may be paid more than a young worker in the hotel or restaurant industry, but both have declining levels of earnings relative to older workers in their respective industries.[10] The shift into low-paying sectors of the economy has been greater for young workers than for older workers, which may partially account for the pattern, but again the shift does not appear to be the main factor.

Studies by Statistics Canada have found an increasing polarization of hours worked among men.[11] Some men are working more hours and others are working fewer, while the number of those working a standard workweek has been declining. Moreover, workers with high hourly wages tend to be working more hours, and those with low hourly wages tend to be working fewer hours. This polarization in hours worked accounts for part of the divergence of male earnings in Canada, in combination with the changes in hourly wage rates.[12] A similar shift away from a standard workweek towards both longer and shorter hours has occurred among women, but with a difference. Women working part-time have increased the number of hours they work much more than women working full-time. This has brought the lower level of earners closer to the middle and upper levels, decreasing the degree of inequality among women. The pattern reflects the increased participation of women in the labour force; overall more women are working, and those working part-time are working more hours per year. Women working full-time, however, are less likely than their male counterparts to work a lot of extra hours.

A number of pressures work more against new entrants to the labour market than against those who are already employed and protected by collective agreements or the personnel policies of their employers. Employers, both public and private, may have favoured older workers as they went through the downsizings and delayerings of the 1980s and 1990s, reducing entry-level wages for younger workers while maintaining or increasing the wages of older workers.[13] At the same time, they may have chosen to employ younger, less experienced, and less skilled workers on a part-time or temporary basis while maintaining a core of experienced permanent staff, or they may have contracted out less skilled work to smaller, non-unionized firms that hired only just-in-time workers and paid them lower wages. This could account for the correlation of high wages with increased hours, and of low wages with decreased hours, as well as of low wages with younger workers. Employers may have disincentives to hiring new workers because of higher payroll taxes, such as CPP and employment insurance, and higher training costs due to technological change, which may lead them to demand extra hours from existing employees rather than hire new ones. As well, pressure on employers to keep employment costs down has increased with the opening of Canada's economy to free trade with the United States and Mexico, more liberalized trade with the rest of the world under the new trading regime of the World Trade Organization, and funding reductions in the public sector.

The continuing high rate of youth unemployment in Canada and the rapid increase in the proportion of young workers with postsecondary education have also made it easier for employers to hire younger workers at lower rates of pay even though they are better educated. Unemployment also adds to the age-based earnings gap, because younger workers have a higher unemployment rate; they move in and out of unemployment much more frequently than do older workers, thereby further reducing the number of hours they work in a year.

In an environment of increased competition in the private sector as well as public-sector funding cuts, then, employers are under pressure to keep their employment costs down. The methods they have chosen tend to work to the disadvantage of younger workers, offering them not only fewer hours of work both weekly and annually but also lower hourly wages for the hours that they do work. This applies across all industries, occupations, education levels, and regardless of union membership. A shift in employment opportunities for many younger workers to lower-paying industries may also explain part of the trend. At the same time, the gender earnings gap is closing because the age-based earnings gap is greater for men than for women. The reason that young women are not losing ground to older women in the same way as young men are to older men seems to be that they are working more hours, per week and per year, than their predecessors did. In the case of women, therefore, the pattern is explained more by the behaviour of female workers than by the behaviour of employers.

The earnings trends for both young women and young men are long-term tendencies and should stabilize. When they do, young men will have lower relative earnings than in the past, but some will be able to look forward to steep increases as they age. In other words, the pattern of lower lifetime earnings for each successive cohort of young men as they age has to come to an end at the point when the new employer practices have been in place for a generation. Some men (and possibly women) who are young now will eventually move into those privileged positions now occupied by older men. The earnings of young women will come to resemble those of young men; they will be low relative to older women, but closer to those of men of the same age and education level, and some university-educated young women should also have large increases in earnings as they age.

In the end the people who will achieve large increases in earnings as they age will be those who are paid more per hour and who work more hours. Apart from freelance consultants and business owners, these will be people who work in the primary labour market, in the shrinking core of secure jobs with good wage levels and benefits, or as independent professionals in fields with a high demand for help. Unless changes come in the gender division of labour in unpaid domestic roles, or with a large-scale provision of child care as a public good, men will still be more likely to work longer hours. They will also be more likely to have unbroken careers and therefore more likely to move into the highly paid core of permanent employees as they age. Both factors will tend to widen the gender earnings gap as each cohort ages.

It is more difficult to predict which industries and occupations will have the steeper increases in earnings. It seems safe to say that an occupation requiring a postsecondary degree, diploma, or certificate will pay more over the lifetime of the worker, but there is no guarantee that any particular investment in formal skills training and credentials past high school will bring rewards. Despite talk of the growing "knowledge economy," the difference between the earnings of university-educated and high-school-educated young workers in Canada has shown little change. This is probably because there has been such a rapid increase in the proportion of well-educated youth that employers do not have to pay a premium for them, and many are underemployed in jobs that do not make use of their training. In the United States, by contrast, there is a growing earnings gap based on educational credentials.[14] It seems likely that this will begin to occur in Canada too, with the ongoing polarization of the labour market into highly skilled, well-paid jobs and low-paid, low-skill jobs.

The earnings pattern of the future will be based on a complex interaction of age, gender, and education, with the type of education achieved influenced largely by social-class background. Young workers will start out with relatively low incomes, but if young men and women marry or live together (in same-sex or opposite-sex couples) they will be more likely to have two incomes for a longer period of time, and if their lives proceed according to their plans they will continue to have two incomes for most of the years after having children. Over a lifetime, the real basis of inequality will be the value of their skills and educational credentials in the labour market. Inequality based on age and gender will still be a part of life, but class origin and education will underlie the major social and economic divisions.

><><

Declining earnings and incomes have changed the typical life experiences of young people. Some speculate that we may be moving to life-course patterns similar to those of the nineteenth century, when most people began their independent working lives in poverty, grew more prosperous in middle age, and lapsed again into poverty in old age.[15] Canadian society has reduced poverty among the elderly over the past twenty years, thanks in particular to the Guaranteed Income Supplement, but the situation of young adults has deteriorated dramatically. Living in poverty has become the norm for young unattached individuals. Almost two-thirds of people under the age of twenty-five who lived on their own in 1996 had incomes below the poverty line, compared to less than half in 1980. For families headed by people under twenty-five, the poverty rate rose from 20 per cent in 1980 to 42 per cent in 1996.[16]

What this means for young people seeking to make the transition to adult independence varies according to their circumstances. For many, perhaps most, the new realities mean a longer period of dependence on their parents. Some must practise an ascetic life style while they combine low-wage work with postsecondary studies. Many young adults who have full-time jobs have to delay home ownership and families of their own while they pay off their student loans.

The burden falls most heavily on young people who are already disadvantaged by impoverished or dysfunctional families. Many families have been injured by the difficult economic conditions of the 1990s. Youth whose parents lack the financial or emotional resources to support them adequately are liable to extreme forms of deprivation, including homelessness, hunger, and disease. They may be forced by the lack of family support and job opportunities into dangerous survival strategies, from panhandling to the sex trade to criminal activity. The young people who dart from street corners to wash windshields for cash while the traffic light is red have emerged as symbols of these marginalized youth. Part waif, part rebel, and part entrepreneur, the squeegee kid has become a feature of downtown life and a litmus test for adult attitudes.

Many authorities are offended by the sight of the squeegee kids. "I would like to see them banned," said one Ottawa city councillor, "because they give the city a bad image and it's dangerous."[17] Others romanticize their initiative and independence. Cities across Canada are debating what to do about squeegee kids in terms that could have been used by Victorian reformers over a century ago.

The squeegee kid controversy is an example of a common social phenomenon that criminologists call a "moral panic" that breaks out periodically around youth.[18] A moral panic links youth's problems of the day, whatever they may be, with adult anxiety over moral laxity, crime, violence, gang behaviour, or political extremism on either the right or left. A problem in society encountered by youth is transformed into a problem residing in youth, a problem that presents a threat to society. We have already seen how bishops and politicians transformed the issue of mass youth unemployment during the Depression into concerns about the spread of "unnatural vices," premarital sex, and the appeal of the Communist Party to youth. When the economy heated up a few years later during World War II and young people were drawn

into the labour market in large numbers, adults suddenly became concerned that young women were becoming too independent, and delinquency was said to result not from idleness but from having too much
cash.

The one constant in these moral panics is the lack of supporting
empirical evidence. The phenomenon breaks out around sensational
media accounts that may or may not be typical of trends for youth generally. Among recent moral panics have been the widespread concerns
about the issue of high-school dropouts at a time when the dropout rate
was declining rapidly and about young offenders when youth crime rates
were also falling.

Public anxiety about youth behaviour and revulsion at the appear-
ance of young people making their living by cleaning windshields at
street corners have co-existed with drastic cutbacks in the level of social
services provided to marginalized youth. Voters have demonstrated their
preference for governments that eliminate deficits and reduce taxes
while cutting back on education and social services. Among the many
risks encountered by today's youth is the declining availability of support to those who are most vulnerable. Marlene Webber, the author of
Street Kids: The Tragedy of Canada's Runaways, concludes: "It is hard
to imagine many kids would be in the street if schools were committed
to educating and guiding students at greatest risk for personal ruin; if
public-assistance programs extended realistic financial support to families and individuals, including adolescents in need; if social service provided family counselling and community-based mental health clinics to
help disturbed youngsters before they hit rock bottom; if the state guaranteed kids loving alternatives to dangerous homes; and if the correc-
tions system were dedicated to rerouting budding delinquents."[19]

But most young people are not exposed to this extreme kind of risk. For
the majority, the consequence of low incomes, long years of schooling,
and rising tuition fees is prolonged dependence. It is common to see
youth in their twenties staying in the family home or returning to it after
a time away. In 1991 about two-thirds of men and women aged twenty
to twenty-four lived with one or both parents, according to the census,
and even in the twenty-five to twenty-nine age group, 44 per cent of
unmarried men and 33 per cent of unmarried women still lived at
home.[20] These figures were only likely to increase during the 1990s as
more young people withdrew from the labour market and stayed in
school. Research shows that the tendency to stay at home with parents

rises in difficult economic times and declines in good times — an effect similar to the one observed in 1850s Hamilton. Most young adults in their twenties who return home to live with their parents after a time away do so for economic reasons. They are returning to school and need support, or they cannot find a job, or if they have a job it is insufficient to support themselves independently, or they are simply living with their parents to save money.[21] It is clear that this generation's transition to adult independence is taking longer than it did for their parents, although not necessarily any longer than it did for the generations who came of age before World War II.

Two University of Western Ontario professors, James Côté and Anton Allahar, argue in their book *Generation on Hold* that this delayed transition to adulthood is harmful to young people. Citing anthropologist Margaret Mead, they begin with the proposition that a society should give young people a clear role to play and a consistent set of beliefs about the world. Far from doing this, they say, industrial societies have disenfranchised young people, taken away any meaningful productive role they may play in society, and instead targeted them as consumers. Young people develop identities not as active producers of value in our society but as consumers either of the leisure industries, such as media and music, or the identity industries, particularly fashion and education. Coming of age now involves developing a self-identity based on an alliance with one of these forces, Côté and Allahar argue. For example, young people may adopt the images manufactured by the leisure industries or base their identities on credentials conferred by the education system. Because these identities lack substance, they say, the result is "an epidemic of socially produced identity crises."[22]

This is a provocative analysis, especially coming from two university professors. They portray their own institution as a consumer industry that targets young people, providing them with illusory foundations for their identity. It is a bold thesis, especially as Canadian universities gear up their marketing strategies to compete for students. Côté and Allahar go on to argue that our society's failure to provide youth with productive roles is creating widespread social unrest, a culture of dissent that will be marked increasingly by collective outbursts. The cover of their book features an image of a pistol and the out-of-focus face of an angry, menacing youth.

Despite their sympathy towards youth, the kind of analysis that Côté and Allahar put forth has the unfortunate effect of feeding stereotypes about youth crime and violence, contributing to yet another moral panic. Côté and Allahar stop short of providing any convincing

empirical evidence for their arguments. The research done on this question suggests that frustrated efforts to find a productive role, particularly
a meaningful job, tend to be experienced in isolation, as personal problems. Rather than leading to dissent through collective outbursts, those
frustrations lead, if anywhere, to withdrawal, apathy, self-blame, and in
extreme cases to addictions and clinical depression.[23] Even in this regard
the evidence is far from adequate. For example, Côté and Allahar report
a "consistent upward trend" in suicide rates among young men as one
of the indicators of the emotional cost of their economic plight, and,
indeed, a careful analysis of the trend shows that there was a dramatic
increase in the male Canadian suicide rate from the early 1960s to the
late 1970s. Since then, however, the suicide rates of men in their twenties have declined slowly from a high of 36 per 100,000 in 1978 to 28
in 1995. The annual rate for young men aged fifteen to nineteen
reached 21.5 in 1982 and has since stabilized at around 20.[24]

The suicide of any young person is a tragedy, and many of those
deaths may have been caused by the despair of young people confronted
by a society that seemed to have no place for them. The problem is, we
don't know if this is the main cause, a contributing factor, or a relatively
minor one. If it is an important cause, then surely we would have seen a
further increase during the recession of the early 1980s and the jobless
1990s.

Perhaps more social research would help us understand the effects
of the prolonged dependence of youth. Some analysts argue that unemployment and underemployment do not create the same degree of hardship for youth as they do for prime-age adults, because young people do
not have dependents to support, they can always return to school, or
they are simply more resilient and optimistic. In the absence of research,
any point of view is just a matter of opinion.

The more straightforward argument about this issue insists that the
prolonged dependence of youth is a further source of disadvantage to
those without family resources to fall back on. Parents have varying
degrees of capacity and willingness to support their children through
extended transitions. Research on this question has shown that young
adults are more likely to be living at home if their parents are still
together. Children of divorced or separated parents are less likely to live
with them, especially if the parents have remarried.[25] Cultural differences can play a part: children of parents who value the nuclear family,
and their roles and relations within the family, are more likely to receive
parental support.[26] So too can economic differences: families with fewer
resources simply have less to offer their children, whether they are living

at home or apart. In this light, the prolongation of dependence can serve to increase social inequality. After all, a large part of the rationale for the increases in public spending on postsecondary education in the 1960s and 1970s was to promote social equality. Now, at the very time that a postsecondary education has become critical to a young person's future prospects, and extended years of dependence are required to complete a degree or diploma, governments have been cutting back their support and allowing tuition costs to rise. Families are expected to step in and fill the gap left by these cutbacks.

Even in the best of times, when tuition fees were low, youth from low-income families experienced not only financial but also non-financial barriers to further education, including, often, a lower level of the cultural capital that better-educated parents are able to pass along to their children and the greater likelihood of being streamed into terminal programs in high school. This educational disadvantage now translates into severely reduced employment opportunities. As the cost of prolonged years of education climbs and the labour market polarizes into good and bad jobs, the education system seems once again to be an institution that perpetuates and accentuates social divisions, not one that reduces them.

Youth who are members of disadvantaged groups accumulate further disadvantages due to the necessity to go through a prolonged period of dependence. For example, young people who live in rural areas and small towns are rarely able to live at home when they enrol in a college or university. In addition to the possible emotional cost of leaving their home communities, they must also bear the additional financial expenses that come with living away from home. Living expenses can easily exceed tuition costs. Aboriginal youth already have low rates of high-school completion and participation in postsecondary education due to a history of abusive residential schools and inadequate educational facilities in their own communities. The result has been high rates of unemployment and dependency for them. The demand for increased years of schooling raises the bar and makes it more likely that aboriginal youth will continue to have low incomes and low status in Canadian society. The same can be said for youth with disabilities and those from disadvantaged visible minority groups — those with African, South Asian, and Latin American backgrounds. In short, in the absence of special programs of support for disadvantaged students and their families, the prolongation of youth contributes to the entrenchment and deepening of social divisions in Canada.

Difficulties in coming of age have an impact on the relative status of young men and women and on relations between the sexes. Young women have shown a rapid increase in the level of educational attainment. They are more likely to complete secondary school, and they now outnumber young men at the undergraduate level in universities. More women have non-traditional occupations, especially better-educated women who enter professional and managerial jobs.[27] But the educational choices, occupations, and earnings of young women and men in Canada still display major differences. Men and women still tend to find occupations "appropriate" to their sex, and women's jobs typically pay less.

Women continue to provide most of the child care for young children. This leads to disruptions in women's careers, loss of earnings due to intervals away from work, and, as women age, a widening of the earnings gap, even among university graduates. Women also continue to do significantly more unpaid work in the home than men. A recent study for the Canadian federal and provincial ministers on the status of women estimated that, on average, women put in about one-third more unpaid work in the home than men. When the statisticians count all work, both paid and unpaid, they find that women work an average of 8.9 hours per day to men's 8.3 hours. Counting only paid, full-time work, women earn about seventy-three cents for every dollar earned by men; but including all work, both paid and unpaid, women earn only fifty-two cents for every dollar earned by men. Granted, this method does not account for choices made jointly by couples about the balance of paid and unpaid work that each partner will take on or for how they might choose to redistribute income in the household. It does underline the fact that unpaid work is real and necessary and that women still bear a disproportionate share of it despite their increasing participation in the labour market. The study's co-ordinator noted that women could achieve economic equality with men in one generation if they stopped having children and replicated the work patterns of men, but, of course, without children the society and its economy would soon come to an end.[28]

Women, then, are approaching male levels of labour-force partici-pation, but still carry an extra burden of work in the private sphere of home and family. The need to juggle roles leads to additional conflicts and pressures in their lives. In their book *Lives of Their Own*, a team of Canadian researchers studied the impact of this change on women's lives in the 1980s.[29] They found that women had a greater variety of roles and statuses in their lives than men — a greater range of full-time and part-time statuses as student, worker, spouse, and parent — and a greater fluidity of movement between them throughout their life courses. This made their life courses much less predictable than that of previous generations of women. Men's lives have changed, too, they found, but not as much. Changing gender roles, the prevalence of divorce, the demand for increasing levels of education throughout a career, and labour-market insecurity all combine to make the lives of both sexes more uncertain. But compared to women, men's lives are still more likely to approximate the classic linear progression — complete education, enter the labour market, and work there on a full-time basis until retirement. Women's lives are much less certain and more subject to greater liabilities from labour-market discrimination and career inter-ruptions. The facts that half of all marriages end in divorce and that fewer couples are marrying in the first place put both sexes in jeopardy of having their domestic lives shattered, but divorced women run a much greater risk of having low incomes and living in poverty than do divorced men.

These findings carry several implications for young women. For both economic and personal reasons, most young women plan to have careers throughout their lives, interrupted only by periods spent out of the labour market for childbirth and child care. The pressure on young women to bring in an income has increased further because of the declining level of male incomes and the demise of the concept of the family wage. Men are no longer identified as sole breadwinners. But woman also need to have careers for the sake of their own security as individuals, and young women recognize this. Most invest a great deal of money and years of their lives in a postsecondary education and expect to have a job with good income and status.

To reduce the risk that parenthood presents to the career plans of young women, the logical choice is to postpone childbearing. The optimum sequence of stages for the transition to adulthood, for both women and men, would appear to be completing an education, at least to the level that would allow entry into a planned field of work, getting started on a career-track job, and only then committing to a relationship that might lead to parenthood. A young person might have an independent household and a cohabiting partner before beginning a career-track job, but it would seem prudent for a young woman in particular to have experience in her chosen field before taking time out of the labour market to have children. Considering the prolonged years of schooling and the difficulties of getting started in career jobs, this would mean postponing children until at least her late twenties, more likely her thirties.

Perhaps the greatest single hazard for a young woman is to have a child and become a single mother before she has completed her education. Unless she receives a high level of support from her parents, she will have neither the time nor the resources to continue her education and will have nothing to look forward to for several years but some combination of social assistance and low-wage jobs. Households headed by single mothers account for a high percentage of the population living below the poverty line in Canada.

A strictly rational choice, the kind that economists are fond of, would dictate that young people should not plan to have children at all. Children are an economic burden, demand large quantities of unpaid labour time, and increase women's vulnerability in the labour market. Not surprisingly, women are having children later in life, compressing the period of time they are out of the labour market with preschoolers, and simply having fewer children. Canada's fertility rate, the average number of births per woman in her lifetime, has dropped steadily since the 1960s and now stands at 1.64, well below the society's replacement level. Demographers tell us that a fertility rate of 2.1 is necessary to replace the existing population: one child for each parent and a further 0.1 for children who do not survive to adulthood.[30]

Certain options could reduce the pressure on women and make it easier for them to combine roles as workers and mothers. It is neither reasonable nor realistic to expect women to revert to traditional gender roles. That choice may be available to some who are in secure relationships with partners who earn an adequate family income, but changing expectations and economic necessity do not allow it for most. To some extent the pressure can be reduced within a relationship if the parenting and other domestic tasks are shared more equally with men. It can also be eased by changes in the practices of employers to allow part-time work, working from home, and child care in the workplace. Families with higher incomes can afford to hire nannies and housekeepers to do their domestic work, and this is the option chosen by large numbers of couples when both partners have professional careers. Child-care expenses can be partially recouped through tax refunds, but this is a benefit only to those who can afford to pay these expenses in the first place. Many families in which both parents have jobs rely on day care, whether public or private, but subsidized day-care spaces are in short supply and have dwindled in many places as governments cut back social spending. A publicly funded child-care system available to all families who need it would go a long way towards resolving the problem. As it is, Canada has a low level of public support for working mothers. This makes the lives of women who cannot afford private domestic staff or day care much more pressured and vulnerable than the lives of those with higher incomes and well-paid partners.

Knowledge of these facts feeds back into the plans and decisions of young women, motivating them to go further in their education, to aim for well-paying careers with "family-friendly" employers, and in the meantime to postpone childbearing until later in their lives. Young women who deviate from these new norms face a much greater risk of low incomes and pressured lifestyles.

Social divisions are deepened by the phenomenon of "assortative mating." As the job market becomes more polarized, people have a greater tendency to choose partners with similar levels of education and income. One sad twentysomething university graduate who had been unable to find a job equal to his educational qualifications wrote to *The Globe and Mail* about his problems. The most common phrases in the Companions Wanted ads, he complained, were "financially secure," "well-established," "professional," and "accomplished." He continued with several of his personal experiences, for example:

Last summer I met a woman during the Terry Fox Run. For five kilometres I struggled to keep pace with both her stride and conversation as she bounced along easily beside me. She seemed genuinely interested in having a new running partner until our gasping and fitful jogger's discussion came around to what we'd been doing since school. After hearing her story, I told mine. Before long the next water station provided a rest for me and a chance for her to keep right on going. I never did catch up with her. She's probably still running.

He concluded that, more than ever, a companion is an economic ally. "As if love itself had yielded to the market," he wrote, "each person looks for prospective mates with rational self-interest."[31]

Adding to the psychological misery, assortative mating doubles the disparity between households at different levels, contributing to the growing gap between rich and poor families. Statistics Canada reports that this gap continued to grow in 1996 despite that year's strong economic performance. The average yearly income of the bottom fifth of families fell from $17,882 to $17,334, while the average income of the richest fifth rose from $112,822 to $114,874. The income earned by the poorest fifth of families fell to 6.1 per cent of Canada's total income, while that of the richest fifth rose to 40.6 per cent, higher than at any time in the 1980s and 1990s and higher than the bottom 60 per cent of Canadian families combined. This state of affairs continues a trend that has been going on since the 1970s: the rich families getting richer while the poor get poorer. Most families reach the top fifth only by combining two professional incomes. The disparity would be even more dramatic if the calculations included only earnings from employment, because the inequality is moderated somewhat by social transfers such as unemployment insurance, old-age security, child tax credits, and welfare payments. The cutbacks in these programs across Canada — particularly in eligibility for unemployment insurance and reductions in welfare benefits — have been part of the explanation for the growing disparity in family incomes.[32]

Not surprisingly, young people respond to this growing inequality of family incomes by holding out for partners who can be economic allies. But once they are partners their problems have just begun, for now they must find ways to co-ordinate the demands of the labour market with the needs of their relationship. The increased freedom from traditional roles and commitments makes every individual, male and female, more dependent on the labour market for personal security. The liberation of women in particular from traditional roles also separates them from traditional commitments and security, a risk that motivates the activism of conservative women in organizations like REAL Women. In the labour market, young men and women find their lives increasingly individualized. Among the most common issues arising in relationships are the questions of where to live and of whose job comes first. For many, especially young workers just beginning career-track jobs, the answer is to live apart. This further delays committed relationships and limits the space available for private, personal life. The labour market — its demands, its cycles, its risks and opportunities — becomes the dominant fact of life.

7
Policy Responses to Labour-Market Problems

"*D*o you have any idea, Mr Chrétien, how a job is created in a modern economy?" The Reform Party leader, Preston Manning, finger raised like a pedantic schoolmaster, posed this challenge to the prime minister in the televised leaders debate of the 1997 general election. Chrétien replied that his government had attacked unemployment by addressing "the fundamentals" — reducing the deficit and keeping inflation and interest rates low. This was the way to encourage investment and create jobs, he said. He might have added that his government was doing it by the book. "Set appropriate macroeconomic policy" is the leading policy recommendation of the influential OECD *Jobs Study* of 1994, which went on to outline precisely the points mentioned by Canada's prime minister.[1]

Perhaps if he had prepared more thoroughly for the question, Chrétien could also have rhymed off the other eight recommendations of the OECD *Jobs Study*. These can be reduced to two general strategies: Plan A is to promote the growth of highly productive, high-wage employment to the greatest extent possible, while Plan B is to support the expansion of low-wage employment to reduce the jobless rate among those who are left out by Plan A. High-wage jobs are to be fostered through the promotion of research and development and the diffusion of new technology and by support for formal education and job training. Although new technology may eliminate jobs in the short run, the OECD advises, it will increase productivity and raise the incomes of those in high-skill jobs.

Meanwhile, under Plan B, labour costs are to be reduced in less productive jobs by lowering or eliminating minimum wages and "taxes on employment" such as unemployment insurance premiums and pension plan contributions. When labour costs paid by employers sink low enough, there will be sufficient jobs for all who want them. Of course, these measures need to be accompanied by parallel reductions in unemployment insurance benefits and social assistance in order to remove disincentives to workers to accept low-wage jobs.

At first sight Plan A and Plan B may appear to be competing strategies, but they are complementary. The OECD seems to accept that even in the highly industrialized countries not enough high-wage work will exist for everyone in anything less than the long run. The question, then, is what to do about those who are left out. Their incomes could be supported by strong minimum-wage legislation, but this would interfere with the operation of the labour market. "Wages," says the OECD, "have an important allocative role to play in labour markets by providing clear signals to workers and firms."[2] An alternative would be to reduce working time to spread high-wage employment around, and the OECD does recommend some measures to increase voluntary part-time work. But its main strategy for reducing the unemployment rate is to allow the growth of low-wage jobs.

Here again Esping-Andersen's distinction between the liberal welfare state, the corporatist welfare state, and the social-democratic welfare state comes into play.[3] The OECD's labour-market recommendations are intended to move its member countries in the direction of the liberal model. They are neo-liberal in the precise sense of the term: they advocate a regime in which labour markets are guided by price signals and state interference in the functioning of these signals is minimized. The aim of the original designers of the welfare state was to decommodify labour by insulating citizens from the insecurity inherent in the fluctuations of the labour market. The neo-liberal model reverses this direction, based on the argument that this kind of state interference raises labour costs and hence creates unemployment. The main role assigned to the state in a neo-liberal regime is to promote the competitiveness of its national economy through support for technological development, education, and training. Otherwise, it should deregulate the labour market and get out of the way.

Canada and the other liberal welfare states are in a better position to adopt the OECD's recommendations than the corporatist and social-democratic welfare states, which have entrenched class interests involved in preserving the status quo. But high unemployment rates in the corporatist states and fiscal problems in the social-democratic states are pushing them in the neo-liberal direction. In the current international economy, policy managers seem to have only two choices: high wages with high unemployment, and low wages with low unemployment. Each approach has its distinctive problems, but the industrialized countries are showing a growing official consensus that a substantial low-wage sector is the lesser of two evils.

The communications strategy accompanying this direction highlights Plan A. In Canada this approach has been labelled the "competitiveness agenda." It first appeared in the late 1980s and early 1990s as Canada was coming to grips with the effects of the push to free trade and broader global competition. Its message is this: in the new era of global competition Canada started from a weak position, the result of declining global demand for our natural resources, a century of protecting the manufacturing sector behind a tariff wall, and an expensive but mediocre education system. The state needs to play a critical role in promoting the competitiveness of the Canadian economy in several areas, including support for research and development, promoting technological change, and improving the level of skills in the workforce. In the global economy, the advantage goes to the country with the best-trained, most skilled workforce.

Plan A is now the dominant approach to solving the labour-market problems of youth in Canada, especially in the federal government and its agencies. The key tasks of this strategy are to promote a high level of knowledge and skills in areas needed by the economy and to bridge the gap between the education system and the labour market. In education the emphasis is on improving quality, especially in the subjects viewed as most critical to the economy — literacy, mathematics, and science — and on encouraging students to stay in school. Easing the transition from school to work are programs of co-operative education, internships that provide work experience, and youth apprenticeship programs that allow students to complete their high-school diplomas while qualifying for skilled trades.

Education Reform

In the last decade *competition* became a buzzword not just in business circles but also in Canadian education systems. Schools and teachers must compete with their counterparts in Europe and Asia as they prepare the next generation to play its role in the new era of global competition; they must compete between provinces to see whose education system is the best at providing a grounding in the basic skills required in the economy; and students must compete with each other to determine who will get into the university and college programs of their choice.

This drive to competition is fuelled to a large degree by middle-class parents anxious to give their children every advantage they can in a difficult labour market. Their anxiety is understandable. You can't fault parents for wanting the best for their children. This more than anything accounts for the successful appeal of political parties that have been elected to office promising reform of education systems and curricula. Additional pressure to improve employability skills comes from employers. Corporations in the private sector also want to sell more goods and services to education systems, and it is in their interests to raise concerns about the quality of education.

Several major reports in the past decade have addressed the need to improve Canada's education systems, with a recurring theme: the need to raise the level of knowledge and skills in order to compete effectively in the global economy.[4] But not everyone sees it this way. Philip Nagy, a professor at the Ontario Institute for Studies in Education, has identified four important sets of voices in the current debates on education reform.[5] First, the concern of federal agencies about economic competitiveness, he says, has led them to advocate national standards and testing, with a focus on basic skills — first language, mathematics, science — as well as more advanced academic skills — thinking, problem-solving, and technology use. They place much less emphasis on other academic subjects, such as social studies, second languages, the arts, and physical education, and on broader "citizenship" goals, including personal growth and self-confidence — all of which are viewed as less pertinent to employability and more difficult to measure.

Second, business-oriented groups also tend to see the key educational goal as the promotion of Canada's economic competitiveness through the development of employability skills. For instance, the Conference Board of Canada's *Employability Skills Profile* emphasizes academics (communication, thinking, learning), personal management (positive attitudes, responsibility, adaptability), and teamwork, taking a somewhat broader view of education than the federal government's perspective but placing little or no value on the arts, social studies, or physical education.[6]

The education reform movement, the third set of voices, is made up primarily of citizen-based organizations dissatisfied with their education systems. Members are typically taxpayers angry about costs and parents concerned about the quality of education received by their children. They charge that the education system is bureaucratic, lacks accountability, and is not cost-effective.[7] They advocate greater choice for parents through charter schools, voucher systems, or other methods that would give them greater control as parents and citizens. They also tend to advocate eliminating "frills," reducing administration costs, and focusing on "the basics" — communication skills, mathematics, and science. In some provinces, notably Newfoundland, the issue of school choice is closely related to the efforts of religious denominations to have control over their own schools.

The fourth set, education professionals, generally favour a broader view of education goals. They argue that the skills, knowledge, and attitudes needed in society go well beyond those required in the workplace and that, in any case, workplace skills themselves are much broader than usually acknowledged.

Each of these voices represents a political force influencing the main decision-makers in Canada's formal education systems: the provincial and territorial governments, particularly their ministries of education. The provincial authorities have formed a co-operative body, the Council of Ministers of Education, Canada (CMEC), to share information and co-ordinate common projects. In its *Joint Declaration: Future Directions for the Council of Ministers of Education, Canada* in 1993, the CMEC identified lifelong learning and accountability as the two overarching themes for education and training in Canada. The CMEC's First National Consultation on Education in May 1994 arrived at a consensus on the need to ensure greater accountability for student performance in the education system, graduation rates, and successful transitions from school to work. The CMEC initiated the Pan-Canadian Education Indicators Program to monitor a broad range of indicators of performance in the learning system as a whole, including both the formal education systems and job-related education and training. The CMEC has also initiated the School Achievement Indicators Program (SAIP), which measures the achievement of thirteen- and sixteen-year-olds in every province and territory in reading, writing, and mathematics.

Most provinces have carried out extensive studies of their education systems, and many have introduced major revisions requiring

stricter requirements for a secondary school diploma. All now participate in national testing. Provinces have also begun sharing resources and
information to develop common curricula. In short, there is plenty of
evidence of a general concern about connecting education to labour-
market needs and about the need for high-quality education, especially
at the primary and secondary levels. These improvements are important,
because without them increasing numbers of parents would seek individual solutions for their children, undermining the public school system.

Still, many of these debates are reminiscent of the famous Will
Rogers line: "Schoolin' ain't what it used to be, and it never was." The
narrow focus on employability skills and back to basics curricula seems
to be founded on the idea that the school system carried out its function
better in some mythical past. The arts, social sciences, and physical education are also an essential part of an education for life. Moreover, it is
worrisome to see the reintroduction of streaming into secondary
schools, because the streaming of youth into terminal programs has
proved to be a leading cause of their alienation and dropping out.[8]
Research in this area indicates that reducing the distinction between academic and vocational streams is a more productive approach. It reduces
the stigma attached to vocational streams, facilitates movement between
streams, and gives all students a greater range of options in postsecondary studies and in their career directions.[9]

Access to Education

There is no doubt that completing high school and gaining a postsecondary degree, diploma, or certificate enhance the life chances of
young people. These steps are no guarantee, as we have seen, but for
most people the qualifications are a necessary if not sufficient condition
of access to good jobs and decent incomes. In recognition of this, in the
early 1990s the federal government experimented with a stay-in-school
initiative, which included interventions such as mentoring, tutoring,
peer support groups, and parental involvement. The program appeared
to have good results, though this may have been due to the decision of
many young people to stay in school because of the poor labour-market
conditions of the times rather than to the impact of the program itself.

Creating the opportunity for young adults to return to school to
complete their high-school diploma also reduces the rate of non-comple-
tion; older students are likely to be better motivated when they have
experienced the reality of the labour market and made a mature decision
to return to school. Unfortunately, adult high-school programs have

been among the first to disappear when governments and school boards have trimmed their budgets.[10]

There is a strong association between class background and dropping out, perhaps due in part to the difference in the level of resources available to schools in middle-income and lower-income neighbourhoods. Policies that equalize resources to schools in different regions can help, and strong evidence exists to indicate that problems of poor academic performance and dropping out could be reduced by providing early childhood education in the preschool years. A growing body of research shows that development of the brain in the first five years of life has a critical impact on a child's lifelong capacity for thinking, learning, and socializing, which means that early childhood education within a public system could do a great deal to overcome disadvantages caused by poverty or dysfunction in families. In the words of the Ontario Royal Commission on Learning, "Early childhood education significantly helps in providing a level playing field of opportunity and experience for every child, whatever her background."[11] A public system of child care and education staffed by well-trained specialists would also address the problem of working mothers, but absolutely no progress has been made in establishing such a system despite repeated promises by successive federal governments.

The rising cost of postsecondary education has been one of the highest profile youth issues in recent years. As governments have cut back funding for universities and colleges, they have allowed tuition fees to rise, shifting a larger percentage of the cost of education away from the public purse and onto individuals. Rising tuition costs combined with living expenses make it difficult or impossible for many low-income youth to continue their education, and they put an increasing strain on middle-income students as well. About half of all postsecondary students have to borrow money to pay these costs. In his 1998 budget speech, Finance Minister Paul Martin estimated a student's average debt load on graduation to be around $25,000. Students carry this debt into an uncertain labour market: periods of unemployment are common, and the incomes of graduates are much lower than they were a generation ago.

For much of the past decade, the remedy most frequently proposed has been a system of income-contingent repayment loans (ICRLs). In this system, loan repayments are made through the tax system once students are finished school and earning incomes above a certain threshold. The burden remains on individuals, but the level of repayment each year is contingent upon their earnings in that year. The former students can always repay the loan more quickly if they are able to do so. The system is equitable, it is argued, because students are paying a portion of the cost of the education that they have benefited from, and they are repaying their loans at a rate based upon their current income. The problem with ICRLs — and with loans of all kinds — is that rising tuition fees mean students may amass debts that hang over them for decades after graduation. As the Canadian Federation of Students has pointed out, the lower their incomes after graduation, the less their annual payments will be, the longer their payments will stretch out over time, and the more interest they will have to pay. The Federation led an effective campaign against ICRLs after the loans were proposed in a federal discussion paper in 1994, and the government subsequently dropped them from consideration.

Instead, in its February 1998 budget the federal government announced a package of measures known as the Canadian Opportunities Strategy. The measures included improvements to the Registered Education Savings Plan, including a grant of 20 per cent on the first $2,000 of annual contributions, to encourage parents to save for their children's postsecondary education; provisions to increase relief on student loan interest and principal payments under certain circumstances, and tax-free withdrawals from RRSPs to pay education expenses. The centrepiece of the package is the $2.5 billion Millennium Fund, which will provide scholarships averaging $3,000 each year to over one hundred thousand low-income and middle-income postsecondary students.

An alternative federal approach would have been to transfer an equivalent amount through the provinces to universities and colleges, effectively restoring a portion of the amounts chopped from transfers to the education sector in the 1990s. The decision to make the transfers directly to individual students is a significant policy departure. Most of the post-announcement commentary focused on the immediate political motives of the government — its desire to strengthen the visible role of the federal government, and the Liberal Party, in the lives of hundreds of thousands of young Canadians. Much less commentary considered the implications of the shift of such a large amount of funding from institutions to individuals, which represents a new approach to the financing of public institutions. Students who receive scholarships will be entitled to use them at most postsecondary institutions in Canada. This neo-liberal strategy pioneered by Margaret Thatcher to promote competition among public institutions creates the opportunity for private institutions to enter the arena and compete for students on a more equal basis with those receiving public funds. The program reinforces the market model of education.

The Millennium Fund and the other measures in the Canadian Opportunities Strategy should be of some benefit to both low-income and middle-income students and their families, but its full impact remains to be seen. It will do nothing to slow down the rate of tuition-fee increases, and provincial authorities may use it as grounds to reduce their support to postsecondary education and remove all constraints on tuition fees. A few months after the announcement of the Millennium Fund, the Ontario government, for example, stated that it would be deregulating tuition fees for all university postgraduate programs and some undergraduate programs that provide good career prospects, such as computer engineering. In this light, $3,000 scholarships may not do much to ease the burden on students.

Improving School-Work Transitions

Canada's liberal state has never had the tradition of corporatism that, for example, provides Germany's dual system of occupational training with the active support of employers, unions, and the state. Over the past decade, the federal government has promoted the idea of "social partnership" in the labour market, especially for skills training, but with meagre results.[12] This lack of social partnership is seen as one of the key weaknesses in Canada's arrangements for school-work transitions. There is a gap between the education system and the labour market. Many new initiatives in labour-market measures for youth have attempted to bridge this gap with programs that engage the active participation of employers, community-based organizations, educational institutions, and public agencies. Among these initiatives are co-operative education, internships, and youth apprenticeships.

Co-operative education programs place students in jobs with employers as one component of their formal course of studies. The work is jointly supervised by the employer and an academic adviser. Employers may be compensated through tax credits, wage subsidies, or simply by the free or low-cost labour provided by the student.

The purpose of these programs varies according to the level of education. At the secondary school level, a co-op placement is intended to give the student exposure to a chosen field of work. There is no formal training or certification involved. The experience may be part of a larger program of career studies now offered in several provinces, particularly in Western Canada. In other cases, however, there may be little or no follow-up, and a student may simply see the co-op job as an easy credit.

Co-operative education is on the secondary school curriculum in most jurisdictions in Canada, but only 4 per cent of secondary school students opt for it.[13] There are several obstacles to the program's success. Some students and parents doubt the value of co-operative education for college- or university-bound youth and tend to see it as a form of terminal vocational training. Employers, especially smaller businesses and organizations, may be reluctant to offer workplace opportunities to youth because of the extra management time and costs that would be incurred for supervising the youth. Co-workers may see youth in co-operative programs as taking work opportunities away from other insiders. Outside of large metropolitan areas, the variety of workplace experiences in sectors that are likely to provide good career prospects is usually quite limited. For their part, schools may have weak links with employers. Co-operative education programs may clash with the demands of traditional classroom learning, for example in class scheduling. Postsecondary institutions may not recognize course credits earned through co-operative education programs. Finally, labour laws may exclude students from certain kinds of protection, such as workers' compensation benefits for injuries on the job.

Given all of these obstacles, it is not surprising to find that co-operative education programs at the secondary school level have not been very popular. Students who go into co-op programs are less likely to continue their education past high school. It is not clear whether this is due to the impact of the program itself or to the type of students who go into co-op programs. It seems most likely that because co-op programs do not provide credits towards admission to postsecondary education, students intending to continue past high school are more likely to focus on accumulating the required academic credits. Even for those who do not go on to postsecondary education, however, co-op programs do not appear to increase their chances of finding jobs or improving their eventual earnings.[14]

Co-operative education at the postsecondary level has grown rapidly over the past decade. Students work with an employer in a real job, learn through experience and on-the-job training, and begin to develop networks in their field that can help them to find jobs when they graduate. Typically a student spends one semester a year in a co-op placement and two in formal studies.

The co-op programs are most developed for engineering and business students, where the relevance is most obvious to employers in labour-market segments with high demand. Programs for students in the humanities present more of a challenge to program organizers. The main problem for all students is the shortage of employers who are willing to take them on for the work terms. Many end up sitting out their work terms at home or pressing on with their studies and skipping work terms due to the shortage of employment opportunities. Nevertheless, one study shows at least modest benefits in terms of enhanced employment prospects and higher incomes for university graduates who opt for a co-op program in mathematics and science and commerce and economics, though not in engineering.[15]

Internships are placements of unemployed and underemployed high-school, college, or university graduates with employers in their field, typically for periods from a few months to one year. Their objectives are to provide the participating interns with work experience in a career-related field, further develop their skills through on-the-job training and mentoring, and give them the opportunity to begin developing networks in their field.

During the 1990s the federal government launched and expanded several large internship programs. Several federal ministries and agencies now sponsor internships with private firms and non-profit organizations in their respective sectors. Human Resources Development Canada also supports a large-scale internship program called Youth Internship Canada, with an annual budget of $89 million. One component of YIC is operated by the private sector through eighteen industry sector councils, including, for example, the councils for the steel industry, tourism, electric and electronic manufacturing, and aquaculture. The financial and in-kind contributions by employers are estimated to exceed the federal government's contributions. The sector council internships lead to employer-recognized skill certification. By the late 1990s all of these federal programs taken together were supporting over fifty thousand internships over a two-year period. Interim assessments suggested that the programs were having a positive impact.

At the provincial level Manitoba's Partners for Careers program, for instance, matches aboriginal high school, college, and university graduates with entry-level career positions in a partnership involving business, aboriginal leaders, and the provincial and federal governments. Under the program, aboriginal youth receive mentorship from industry leaders and are placed in new entry-level positions in the private sector. The principal objective is to develop working relationships between educational institutions, aboriginal organizations, and the business community.

The private sector has also developed a major internship program. Career Edge was launched in 1996 with the support of some of Canada's largest corporations and has since gained several hundred registered host organizations. Prospective interns must be university, college, or high-school graduates willing to spend six, nine, or twelve months acquiring career experience with a host organization. They approach host organizations directly through the Career Edge web site (http://www.careeredge.org). Career Edge acts as the intern's employer, thus eliminating host organizations' risks associated with severance. Host organizations pay Career Edge a fee to cover the $15,000 annual stipend paid to the intern, payroll taxes, and an administrative fee. Host organizations are also able to place interns outside of their own organization, for example with customers and suppliers or with non-profit organizations. All host organizations and interns sign Career Edge's Code of Conduct and Workplace Practices. Career Edge stipulates that all internships should be both challenging and meaningful, allowing interns to gain general experience and build specific career-related skills. The interns' jobs must be newly created positions and must not replace permanent positions or other education-sponsored programs. The federal government has recently signed on as a host organization willing to take on interns in addition to its own programs.

Youth apprenticeship programs provide an option that allows young students to get started on training in skilled trades without abandoning their secondary school studies. The programs aim to attract more youth, especially women, into apprenticeship programs in order to alleviate skill shortages in specified trades and to correct age and gender balances.

Regular apprenticeship programs have been in decline in Canada for a number of reasons. Occupations with apprentices are concentrated in the traditional trades — manufacturing, construction, and traditional services — which have had weak job growth for more than a decade. Moreover, the cost of apprenticeship training is high, for both the employer and the apprentice. An employer in Canada pays more than three times the amount an employer in Germany would pay, because the term is longer and the minimum wage is higher. At the same time, an apprentice must stay in the program longer and will find the wage low because, on average, the apprentice is much older than a German counterpart — twenty-six years old, compared to an average of sixteen to seventeen in Germany.[16] Youth apprenticeship programs address this problem by getting apprentices started at an earlier age.

Ontario was the first jurisdiction to develop this kind of program. In the Ontario Youth Apprenticeship Program (OYAP), students train as registered apprentices while enrolled in school. The program is open to students who are at least sixteen years of age and have completed Grade 10. They work to complete their secondary school diplomas while also gaining apprenticeship training towards a Certificate of Qualification with journeyperson status in a skilled trade. Students must complete a minimum of three in-school credits per year, and schools must monitor the program offered in the workplace to ensure that it meets their credit requirements: to receive their secondary school diploma, students must still complete all compulsory credits. For the apprenticeship requirements, students must be employed with a qualified employer and fulfil all requirements of an apprenticeship program. They earn a percentage of a journeyperson's wage during the on-the-job portion of the program. Training consultants from the Ministry of Education and Training monitor the students' progress to ensure that industry standards and training requirements are being met. Any students who find that they are not suited to the trade can return to a regular school program after one semester, with no penalty.

Youth apprenticeship programs have been established in five jurisdictions: Ontario, Alberta, Manitoba, British Columbia, and the Northwest Territories. All follow essentially the same model, providing an alternative path into occupations that allow apprentices at a younger age while enabling students to keep open the option of later attending college or university. If they are well planned, youth apprenticeship programs can also focus on skills that are in demand in the local labour market and help to address both labour shortages and skill training needs. Still, youth apprenticeship programs are also expensive, and relatively few young people have decided to register in them. This may be due in part to the low status of such programs in the secondary school culture.

Career Counselling and Labour-Market Information

Effective counselling — education, career, and employment counselling — is an important support to the transitions of individuals through school and work. But in Canada as in other industrial countries, it is unevenly developed and not available to large numbers of young people who need it.[17]

The state of education, career, and employment counselling in Canada has several positive aspects. Materials produced by Human Resources Development Canada are generally regarded as excellent, and so too is the training the agency provides to its employment counsellors. A good deal of energy has gone into creating on-line information that can be used by individuals and agencies across the country (http://www.youth.gc.ca). The quality and availability of guidance in

schools are improving, and particularly so in Quebec, where career guidance counsellors form a professional group with extensive formal preparation. In several provinces, notably Alberta and British Columbia,
career education is an important part of the secondary school curriculum.

The practice also has several limitations. The counselling services of
Human Resources Centres are usually limited to people receiving
employment insurance. Young workers who have left school and are not
eligible for employment insurance may have no access to career counselling apart from expensive private services. Except in Quebec, counsellors in schools usually have limited training for career and employment
guidance and spend half or more of their time dealing with personal and
social issues. Counsellors in other social agencies are, on average, the
least-well trained of all, and their mandate is normally limited to people
receiving social assistance or other designated groups. Many schools and
community agencies lack good resource materials with up-to-date information on the labour market and employment programs at the federal,
provincial, and municipal levels.

International and Canadian studies emphasize the importance of
providing a coherent and comprehensive system of education, career,
and employment counselling that is accessible to all who need it. Agencies and individual counsellors may specialize in providing services to
particular groups, but the system as a whole should be co-ordinated to
provide the full range of education counselling, career education, and
job-placement support required by citizens. The leading Canadian
authorities suggest a "one-start" service for individuals outside the education system, with a single point of entry at which they can be directed
to the appropriate counselling service.[18] Finally, the professional training
and certification of counsellors need to be given higher priority.

Entry-level Workplace Training

Canada lacks a tradition of extensive, formal, entry-level workplace
training for young recruits. Indeed, the country appears to have a lower
incidence of workplace training than does the United States, and the
practice in North America as a whole is surpassed by the programs of
Europe and Japan. For decades the ready supply of skilled immigrant
workers took the pressure off Canadian employers to train their own
workforces in anything but job-specific skills. Training in portable skills
is considered to be the responsibility of the individual and the state.
Moreover, several studies show that most employer-sponsored training

that does exist in Canada goes to prime-age male workers and to those who already have higher levels of formal education.[19]

One method of increasing the level of employer-based entry-level training would be to levy a training tax. Employers would deduct their own training expenditures from their training tax, thus providing a stimulus to employer-sponsored training. The tax would also generate revenue to support state-sponsored training programs. The tax has been advocated by organized labour but resisted by business.[20] It violates the neo-liberal antipathy to any taxes on employment. It would penalize small- and medium-sized employers in particular — and these are the employers who have provided almost all net job creation in Canada in the last decade but also have the least developed training. For small employers the training cost per capita is higher than for large employers because training seems to involve higher fixed costs, expenses that large employers can recoup through economies of scale. Small employers also experience greater disruption when their key employees are absent for training, and they are less likely in the first place to be aware of training opportunities. For these reasons, it seems preferable to use positive measures that make training more feasible for small employers. One proposal is to promote training networks through community-based and sectoral training councils that bring together the business community, colleges, universities, and the local private-sector training community.[21]

When young workers have difficulty even getting jobs, they lack the very prerequisite for gaining access to workplace training. Those who do have work may be employed in part-time, temporary, or just-in-time jobs, in which training is almost non-existent. Even those who do have permanent, full-time jobs are less likely to have access to employer-sponsored training than older workers. In this working environment there is evidence that younger workers who have left full-time education are engaging in a high level of self-initiated, career-oriented formal education and training without support from their employers. Most of this activity is intended to advance their careers by developing portable skills, not to improve their ability to do their current jobs. It would appear that more individual young workers are developing their skills, or at least their resumés, through self-initiated training than with the help of employer-sponsored training.[22]

><

These, then, are the main tactics adopted by federal and provincial governments to promote a high-skill, high-wage strategy for Canada's

youth. While the tactics, as we've seen, have both strengths and weaknesses, certain general problems also arise with their use.

Plan A conflicts with the macroeconomic strategy of reducing government expenditures. For example, the cuts in the transfers to provinces for postsecondary education over the past decade far outweigh the amount that will be contributed by the Millennium Fund. The federal government is contributing to the long-term transformation of postsecondary education from a public good to a market commodity. Most provinces are following its lead with varying degrees of enthusiasm. Only two, Quebec and British Columbia, are attempting to keep tuition fees within reach of most students. Elsewhere governments are making it more difficult for low-income and middle-income students to obtain advanced qualifications.

A second problem with Plan A is its inattention to the demand side of the labour market. Where will the jobs come from for these better-educated youth? Outside of a few specific fields in the high-tech industries, there is great uncertainty about employment prospects in most fields of study. How do education and training change the demand side of the labour market? Human capital theory — with its claim that increasing the general level of skills in the society expands the production frontier of the economy, building the opportunities for producing new goods and services and thereby contributing to the growth of good jobs — makes partial sense, because without the skills we are never going to have the skilled jobs. But a few other necessary conditions exist for the generation of new jobs besides the availability of skilled workers: capital investment, and markets for the goods and services produced by the skilled workers, to name only two. In the postwar "golden age" of demand management, production and consumption grew in tandem, and rising levels of income ensured an increasing level of aggregate demand for the goods and services produced in the industrialized countries. But that age is over. Now stagnant and declining incomes for a large portion of the population raise the fundamental problem of aggregate demand in the economy. To date the response of Canadian governments has been to concentrate on export markets, on being competitive in global markets; and, sure enough, exports have led economic growth since the end of the recession in the early 1990s. But this trend has not generated sufficient growth in demand for the skills young workers have to offer, outside of certain specialized fields, nor is it likely to do so in the near future.

No evidence exists that any country could achieve high-wage employment for all of its workers even if it were able to guarantee sufficient levels of advanced knowledge and skill for all. Perhaps in the long run this approach will work, but that possibility lies beyond the horizon. This is what leads to Plan B, the strategy for expanding low-wage employment.

Reductions in the Minimum Wage and Taxes on Employment

In Canada critics and analysts have put forth a standard argument for reducing the minimum wage. Restructuring of the labour market has eliminated large numbers of unskilled and semi-skilled jobs in the primary sector and manufacturing, and there are not sufficient alternative jobs elsewhere. Unemployment is concentrated in certain population groups, especially among young workers without postsecondary education. The solution, therefore, is to remove the constraints that governments have placed on the creation of low-skill, low-wage jobs. Reduce or eliminate the minimum wage and payroll taxes — employment insurance, Canada/Quebec Pension Plan contributions, workers' compensation premiums, and other taxes paid by employers — and allow employers to create a host of new low-wage jobs for unskilled and inexperienced youth wherever there may be demand for them.

This argument comes right out of Economics 101: when the market functions freely, the theory states, wages find their own equilibrium level — the level at which the demand for young workers equals the supply. When the government imposes artificial constraints on the market by setting a minimum wage higher than the equilibrium level and by collecting payroll taxes, demand shrinks and unemployment results. Reduce or eliminate the minimum wage and payroll taxes, and unemployment will evaporate.

Along with reductions in the minimum wage and payroll taxes, this approach would also reduce or eliminate income tax on low-wage earners, enough possibly to leave them with more take-home pay than they would have had before. Not only would individuals at the low end of the wage scale have more after-tax income, but also the reduced unemployment rate would mean a higher aggregate income for this group as a whole.

The editorial board of *The Globe and Mail* is one of the leading advocates of this approach. Arguing for reductions in the minimum wage and payroll taxes, its members wrote in an editorial on September 17, 1997:

Our true unemployment problem is concentrated among a few identifiable groups, such as young people, the long-term unemployed, and those with few skills needed in the job market. A strategy for dealing with unemployment must therefore be directed at these groups. . . . We need more low-skill, low-wage jobs, not fewer. Getting people into a job, any job, is far more important to their self-respect and their economic prospects than forcing them either to wait for a more interesting and well-paid job that may never come or to take expensive but too-often-worthless job training. One becomes a worker by working. One's value as a worker rises with the experience and skills acquired on the job. . . . Politicians who genuinely care about the plight of the unemployed will brave misguided popular prejudice against "McJobs" and create the conditions in which low-wage work flourishes.

In the same editorial *The Globe and Mail* acknowledges that for its proposals to work the level of welfare and unemployment benefits would also have to be reduced. Otherwise people would have no incentive to go out and work for such low wages or to move from their homes in high-unemployment areas to other parts of the country with more job opportunities. It also freely admits that the wage levels of workers earning above the minimum wage, particularly unionized workers, would be undermined by its proposals. The editors clearly consider this a good thing.

Minimum wages in Canada are legislated at the provincial level. Across Canada they range from below $6.00 to a high of $7.15 an hour in British Columbia. Two provinces — Ontario and Alberta — have subminimum rates for students under the age of eighteen. All other jurisdictions have eliminated their subminimum wages for students, some attributing this to the Canadian Charter of Rights, which prohibits discrimination on the basis of age. Certain occupations in which youth tend to be employed — especially food and beverage servers — also have subminimum wages in Quebec and Ontario, but this is because the workers earn a large part of their income from tips.

Minimum-wage legislation is meant to ensure a living wage and to reduce the incidence of poverty. It also supports the wage levels of workers earning above the minimum wage; their wage position would be undercut by competitive pressures if the minimum wage was reduced, especially at a time of high unemployment. For these reasons, reduction or elimination of the minimum wage is politically unpopular in Canada, and no jurisdiction has attempted it so far. Alberta reviewed its policy on the minimum wage in 1998 with a view to reducing it, but when a public survey revealed that 86 per cent of Albertans favoured an increase, the government reversed itself and decided to raise the minimum wage in stages from $5.00 to 5.90 per hour.

All provinces, however, have allowed their minimum-wage levels to be eroded by inflation since the late 1970s. In most provinces minimum wages are worth only half of what they were twenty years ago. A U.S. study shows that the decline in the real value of the minimum wage through the 1980s contributed to increasing wage inequality in that country.[23] No doubt the same has happened in Canada.

Economists disagree about the real effects of minimum-wage legislation on employment and incomes in general, and on youth in particular. A study in the United States asserts that increases in the minimum wage do not lead to any loss of jobs.[24] This contention challenges neoliberal orthodoxy and has sparked a debate among professionals in the United States and Canada on the question. The Canadian evidence is scanty, but studies suggest that jobs are indeed lost when governments increase minimum-wage rates, especially for those whose earnings are at or near the minimum level before an increase. That group is not large. The percentage of jobs paying the minimum wage is low, ranging from 1.5 per cent in Alberta to 7.5 per cent in Saskatchewan, with an average of 2.5 to 4 per cent for Canada as a whole. Since about half of minimum-wage jobs are part-time, the percentage of "full-time equivalent" minimum-wage jobs is only about 1.6 per cent.[25] The percentage of youth working for the minimum wage is much higher, however, especially among teenagers. An estimated 15 to 20 per cent of employed teenagers in Ontario and Quebec, and up to 40 per cent in the Atlantic provinces, work at minimum wage.[26] Three separate studies indicate that job losses would result from minimum-wage increases for young workers who are currently working for wages at or near the minimum wage, and these losses would probably surpass the break-even point. That is, the group as a whole would suffer a loss of income despite the higher wages of those who retained their jobs.[27] By inference, it is reasonable to expect that there would be employment gains for young workers, especially teenagers, by a decrease in the minimum-wage level and possibly a gain in earnings by the group as a whole despite lower wage rates for individuals.

The OECD's recommendation is that statutory minimum wages be replaced by "more direct instruments" for achieving equitable income redistribution.[28] The method usually put forth is some form of wage subsidy provided by the state, perhaps in the form of a guaranteed annual income or a negative income tax. The principle underlying a negative income tax is the same as that for Canada's Child Tax Credit —

that is, a credit that is gradually taxed back as income rises. Put most simply, below a certain wage level workers receive subsidies from the government; above that level they pay taxes to the government. The program can be restricted to people who are working in wage jobs to provide an incentive to accept such work, or it can be established as an income subsidy, a guaranteed annual income for all, employed and unemployed alike.

A negative income tax would shift the burden of maintaining a living wage from employers to the state, but its cost represents a key problem. Even current levels of the minimum wage are insufficient to keep individuals out of poverty. One estimate of the wage subsidies that would be necessary in the United States just to restore wage differentials to what they were in the mid-1980s amounted to 4 to 5 per cent of GDP.[29] Here again a potential solution conflicts with the macroeconomic policy of fiscal constraint. Even if a guaranteed annual income or negative income tax were introduced, it would provide abysmally low levels of subsidy while justifying a reduction or elimination of minimum wages. Moreover, it would encourage the expansion of low-wage and part-time employment.

Labour-Market Training for Youth

"Labour-market training" is the term used for special government-supported programs that provide job skills for people experiencing difficulties in the labour market. In principle, it could be part of a Plan A strategy — for example, by retraining skilled prime-age workers in a declining industry to move to skilled jobs in a new growth industry. In practice, labour-market training for youth in Canada is concentrated on providing basic job skills for those with low levels of education.

There is a strong trend across Canada towards making it compulsory for any young person receiving social assistance either to return to school or to participate in a labour-market training program. Critics speak of this as "learnfare" or "schoolfare" and see it as part of the broader workfare ideology that coerces people to work in return for income assistance.[30] Workfare is commonly associated with right-wing regimes like Ontario's Harris government, elected on a platform that included a call for workfare and that seemed to blame unemployed people for their plight. But governments of all stripes are reluctant merely to provide passive income support to young people who cannot find work. Even the NDP government of British Columbia, which gives youth employment high priority, makes it clear that young people will not be permitted to collect passive income assistance without actively searching for work or participating in training programs. Social-democrats call this "positive welfare" and speak of the importance of promoting a sense of individual responsibility to counteract the tendency of the welfare state to encourage dependence.[31] The "New Labour" government of Tony Blair in Britain has begun giving jobless youth the choice of finding jobs on their own or entering training programs. After a four-month program, a participant will be placed with a company in the private sector, given work with the government, put on an environmental task force, or enrolled in full-time education or training. One option not available is simply to collect government benefits.[32]

Some Canadian labour-market training programs make use of the formal education system. Others are provided at government expense by private-sector trainers, community-based organizations, or directly by employers. Most programs are not segregated by age group, but young people make up a large portion of the participants.

Governments, both federal and provincial, have developed a wide range of approaches to labour-market training in their efforts to find methods that work. (Until recently, the federal government has played a leading role because of its access to large quantities of special training money allocated from the unemployment insurance fund, but this role and the supporting funds are now being transferred to the provinces.) Many of these programs have received bad publicity for spending large quantities of cash on programs that have been of little value in the search for lasting work. But some approaches have been reasonably successful at getting unemployed youth into low-wage jobs.

A typical program is designed for unemployed people with low levels of formal education and a lack of marketable skills — people called "employment-disadvantaged." Youth account for a large portion of the clients, but labour-market restructuring has left many prime-age workers in this situation as well. Women returning to the labour market after a period of absence for child-rearing also frequently need support for re-entering the workforce.

Most labour-market training programs in Canada have generated only modest gains in employment and income for their participants.[33] They are most effective when combined with other services such as counselling and career information, job search assistance, work experience placements, and various forms of wage subsidy. This suggests that the other factors may be the more useful elements of successful programs. Multifaceted programming, in which the strategy for each individual is developed with some combination of these elements, is now the preferred method for programs intended for disadvantaged youth who face multiple barriers to employment.

The key success factor in labour-market training programs appears to be building strong links to the local labour market. Programs that give emphasis to on-the-job training with real employers, as opposed to classroom training unrelated to a particular workplace, have better results.[34] A "work first" approach is now the method of choice because of its strong connections to local demand. The method used is to begin by finding a job with a local employer and then to subsidize on-the-job training. Academic upgrading takes place at the same time as vocational training, and both are related to the context of the actual job.

Another recent trend in labour-market training is an increased emphasis on entrepreneurship. Most provinces now offer entrepreneurial skills training as well as modest business start-up loans, loan guarantees, and grants. Training and capital assistance are sometimes combined in the same program. Quebec also offers young people training, access to credit, and capital grants to establish farms. Several provinces offer small loans to assist students to start up their own enterprises for summer employment.

Self-employment makes sense in a time when large firms are shedding staff and outsourcing many of their functions. Most new job creation in Canada is by small firms. But there has not yet been much systematic evaluation of the effectiveness of this approach. When programs have reported on the numbers of new businesses and jobs created, the results appear to be low. Moreover, it is not clear whether these initiatives really offer viable alternatives for youth or if they are just another source of low-paying, insecure jobs.

Critics of labour-market training programs point out that the projects do little or nothing to improve the demand side of the unemployment problem, and they say that at best the projects simply increase the competition for jobs and move unemployment around. Advocates argue that training attracts new employers and their investment dollars, although typically to low-paying jobs. The strategy of using skills upgrading to attract telework jobs to New Brunswick is a good example. Supporters also point out that the gains both to individuals and society from training programs accrue over long time periods and that the programs are certainly preferable to unemployment and social assistance.

In short, at least some progress has been made in introducing effective methods of training for young workers to get them into low-wage jobs.

Job Creation

Until recently, direct job creation by the government has been one acceptable form of unemployment relief, whether for young people or any unemployed workers. The measure has usually been a temporary one providing demand for labour during a period of difficulty. Canada's Opportunities for Youth program of the 1970s is a good example. It appeared as the crest of the baby-boom generation was coming of age and entering the labour market. The program funded initiatives proposed by individuals or groups of youth to carry out socially useful tasks, everything from environmental clean-up to theatre. The approach fell into disfavour, though, because it did little to achieve permanent jobs and tended to create dependency on continuing government funding.

With a few exceptions, most youth employment programs in Canada are now designed with training objectives in mind. Even programs designed simply to generate summer jobs for students are justified on the grounds that they provide much-needed income in a period of rising education costs. Some summer employment programs now offer payment in the form of credits against tuition fees at postsecondary institutions. Moreover, an increasing number of temporary job programs for youth emphasize work experience in career-related placements that allow young workers to develop their skills, build their resumés, and begin building personal networks in their field. They are similar in this way to the internship approach and fit into the Plan A strategy.

The federal government's Youth Service Canada (YSC) spends $50 million annually to provide work experience and self-employment opportunities for five thousand youth aged eighteen to twenty-five who do not have postsecondary qualifications and are unemployed and out of school. The 1998 federal budget projected a doubling of these figures to $100 million and ten thousand youth annually. The program works in partnership with community-based employers in the private, public, and not-for-profit sectors across the country to develop community-service projects of various kinds. In addition to gaining work experience, participants receive a weekly stipend and a $2,000 grant that can be claimed when they continue their education, start a business, enter the regular workforce, or pay off a student loan. A job (including self-employment) or a return to school are both considered positive outcomes of the program. A recent survey found that, for every one hundred past YSC participants, sixty-two were employed and twenty-three were in school six to twelve months after completing the program. The remaining fifteen were either unemployed or outside the labour force. Of the sixty-two employed, forty-three were working more than thirty-five hours a week, at one job or a combination of jobs. Only fourteen were earning more than $20,000 annually — or, in other words, working at a rate equivalent to about $11 per hour — while thirty-four were earning between $10,000 and $20,000, and fourteen were earning less than $10,000.[35] What would be necessary — and had not yet been done — was to compare these outcomes with youth of similar backgrounds who did not participate in a YSC program. If the difference were negligible, the YSC program would be open to the charge that it is one more in a string of similar programs, stretching back to the Depression-era Dominion-Provincial Youth Training Programme, that have done little more than "warehouse" unemployed youth. The interim assessment suggests that the YSC has had modest success in encouraging some youth to return to school while moving others from unemployment into low-wage jobs.

><><

Plan B accepts that greater social and economic inequality will be with us for the long run. The suggestion that McJobs provide an entry to the labour market that will eventually lead to better jobs is flawed, given that most low-skill, low-wage jobs are not the first rung on a job ladder. They are dead-end jobs, with little in the way of benefits, training, or career prospects. They are situated in a different part of the labour market, with few links to segments that provide good jobs. Large numbers of well-educated youth are severely underemployed working in these jobs and in danger of losing the skills they have already attained.

Critics of the Plan B approach call it "the race to the bottom," a strategy to compete in the new global marketplace by allowing wages to sink as low as they have to. Canadian political economist Gregory Albo calls it the "competitive austerity" model, contrasting it to the "progressive competitiveness" model, which stresses technological improvements and skills upgrading through heavy investment in education and training, which I have labelled Plan A.[36] Albo sees competitive austerity as typical of a neo-liberal regime and progressive competitiveness as a social-democratic strategy, whereas I have typified the Canadian Plan A and Plan B approaches as two sides of the same neo-liberal coin. It is true that social-democratic welfare states put a great emphasis on education, training, and active labour-market measures designed to achieve full employment, but they go far beyond the level of public investment made in Canada.

Canada lacks the level of social solidarity necessary to support a social-democratic employment strategy for youth. This becomes

evident when we compare the country's efforts to the youth employment policy practised in Sweden during the 1980s.[37] Sweden's policy
was to maintain full employment, and it gave this mandate to a
national Labour Market Board. When youth unemployment began to
rise in the early 1980s, the government established a set of special programs operated through the local branches of the Labour Market
Board. The programs guaranteed every unemployed young person
career counselling, job search and placement services, training opportunities, and a job with a local municipality if all else failed. At the
peak of this effort, Sweden was spending between 2 and 3 per cent of
its Gross National Product on these programs.[38] They were phased out
when the youth unemployment rate receded to about 3 per cent at the
end of the decade.

An equivalent effort in Canada would cost around $20 billion a
year, at least thirty times more than the federal and provincial governments spend annually on all forms of youth job creation and training
outside the education system. Spending of this magnitude demands a
broad social consensus, something Sweden's social-democratic welfare
state has built up in the postwar period, particularly by extending generous benefits to the middle class. That approach has given the majority of
the population a stake in supporting publicly funded solutions to social
problems — solutions funded through high taxes. Canada has never had
a level of publicly funded programs that could be called social-democratic, and the erosion of the principle of universality has undermined
any social solidarity we may have once had. The principal remaining
universal social expenditures that elicit the support of middle-class
Canadians are those going to the health system and public schools. Not
surprisingly, these are now precisely the location of the most intense
political conflicts as fiscal restraint threatens the interests not only of the
poor but also of the middle class.

In Canada the most social-democratic approach to youth is found
in British Columbia, where the NDP government of the 1990s introduced a set of programs and services with the overarching title "A Guarantee for Youth." The strategy includes a freeze on postsecondary
tuition fees, the creation of large numbers of new postsecondary spaces,
and the creation of over twenty thousand jobs and training positions. It
aims to provide a postsecondary space for every graduating high-school
student who wants to continue, but it stops far short of guaranteeing a
job to every young person who needs one. Moreover, British Columbia
might be forced to follow Quebec's lead and begin charging higher
tuition fees to out-of-province postsecondary students.

In a time of market failure, when the private sector has clearly failed to provide adequate levels of employment, income, and security for young Canadians, public policy has failed as well. Canada's neo-liberal direction has undermined social solidarity and encouraged an ethos of competitive individualism. Canadians have learned not to look to the state for solutions. Politicians have learned not to ask tax-payers for more revenue. Public policy, in this time of economic restructuring and dislocation, consists of an inadequate, underfunded set of positive initiatives, a fall-back strategy for expanding low-wage employment, and words of encouragement from our leaders about future economic prospects.

8 Conclusion: Social Solutions and Alternative Approaches

At the conclusion of his *General Theory of Employment, Interest and Money* (1936), John Maynard Keynes expressed his belief that the global unemployment crisis of the 1930s was "inevitably associated with present-day capitalistic individualism."[1] His proposals for restoring a healthy economy without abandoning the free market were to give broad new powers to the state to act on behalf of society to achieve economic stability and full employment. Keynesianism foundered in the 1970s; whether this was due to flaws in the theory or its imperfect application is still debated. Still, given the experience of the past two decades, the reversion to an ideology of competitive individualism is clearly no solution to our social and economic problems. Neo-liberal policies undermine the social solidarity we need to reverse growing rates of poverty and inequality in Canada. They make it especially difficult to create an environment in which young people can achieve independence and become adult contributors to our society.

Young Canadians are coming of age in a society marked by sharper class divisions based largely on the polarization of the labour market. Here the rising aspirations of youth collide with the realities of the new economy, the uncertainty created by new employer practices, the risk of frequent bouts of unemployment, the world of good jobs and bad jobs.

137

The good jobs are challenging, better paid, have better job security, and engage a person's talents and energies. The bad jobs are low-paying, low-skilled, and insecure. Young people are overrepresented in the bad jobs, but many of them can look forward to better opportunities in the years ahead. The long-term problem for individuals who are young now is the risk of being trapped in low-wage, low-skill, insecure employment because of bad decisions or the lack of family resources to support them through longer years of education and difficult transitions to career-track employment. The long-term issue for our society is the prospect of sharper and more deeply entrenched class divisions.

There will always be families who can afford to invest in their children and give them the advantages they need to succeed in a world of competitive individualism. But in a society marked by growing inequality, there will be even more families who cannot make those investments and whose children will be at risk of low incomes, bad jobs, and other threats to their well-being throughout their lives. Private solutions are of benefit only to those who already have an extra share of life's advantages; only social solutions can benefit society as a whole.

It would be unrealistic to put forward an entire platform of social measures that might be adopted by Canadian federal and provincial governments, especially given the much-touted reluctance of politicians and, ultimately, taxpayers to fund these measures. Instead, I would like to briefly present a few ideas for reversing the present neo-liberal direction and attempting to build greater social solidarity around measures that assist youth to make effective transitions to adult independence. A key principle of any strategy is that both low-income and middle-income families must benefit from public policies and programs, for this will be the basis of their social solidarity.

A good starting point is to strengthen the public institutions we already have, beginning with our public education systems. Efforts to improve the quality of elementary and secondary education and to sustain adequate levels of funding for them are critical. Debates will continue about the relative importance of curricula directly related to employability skills versus education as a broader preparation for life. These debates are healthy as long as they take place within the framework of a public commitment to develop a high quality of public education that is available to all. If the public education system deteriorates, increasing numbers of middle-class parents will seek private solutions for their children, and the decline of public systems will accelerate.

It may already be too late to reverse the transformation of post-secondary education from a public good to a private commodity. The conventional wisdom underlying much of the debate on the financing of our universities and colleges is that postsecondary education is of greatest benefit to individuals, and that individual students should therefore be responsible for a much larger share of the expense. Noting with approval the recent massive increases in tuition fees in neighbouring Ontario, the principal of McGill University, Bernard Shapiro, observed, "What it means is that education is not only a public good but it is in a sense a private gain."[2] This reflects the broader neo-liberal position that many of the services we have previously considered to be public goods, available to all on the basis of their common citizenship, should be privatized. In their place the state should offer financial assistance directly to those who need it rather than provide an expensive public service to all.

A pair of British social policy analysts, Robert E. Goodin and Julian Le Grand, advanced this position in their 1987 book *Not Only the Poor: The Middle Classes and the Welfare State*.[3] They pointed out that the middle and upper classes have benefited extensively from the welfare state, while the degree of inequality in society has remained the same or worsened. To overcome this problem of "middle-class capture," they suggested a range of ways to eliminate universality in social programs and focus assistance directly on those with low incomes. In the area of postsecondary education, they argued that major redistributive gains could be achieved by raising fees for postsecondary education and switching from student grants to loans to be repaid out of future income — the well-known idea of income-contingent repayment loans (ICRLs). The savings by government could then be applied to other programs, such as early childhood education, which could benefit disadvantaged youth throughout their school years — a much more significant contribution to social equality than free postsecondary education, they argued.

This is a persuasive argument, but it neglects a vital political point: middle-class taxpayers are reluctant to pay for benefits they do not receive. It is much easier to defend a universal, public health-care system, for example, than it would ever be to win middle-class support for free health care to low-income families while the middle class itself had to pay for its own health services. While middle-income and upper-income youths have long had much higher access to postsecondary education, a system of private postsecondary education with high tuition fees will not resolve this inequality; it will make it worse. From the point of view of society as a whole it would be much more effective to strengthen the status of postsecondary education as a public good available to all citizens and to find alternative ways to reduce the barriers to access encountered by low-income students. Goodin and Le Grand themselves acknowledge that benefits to the middle class are the price of its support.

Moving beyond existing public institutions, we can consider new programs and services that are within the realm of the possible, even in the present political climate. The foremost of these, I believe, is early childhood education. According to two University of Toronto economists who applied a cost-benefit analysis to early childhood education and child care, a public system with well-paid professional staff would cost only half of the amount it would repay to society in improved child development, higher incomes for working women, increased tax revenues, and better life prospects for children. A public program for all Canadian children aged two to five, with a ratio of eight children to each professional staff, would cost $5.33 billion, about five times more than the federal and provincial governments now spend. The total social and economic benefits are estimated to be worth $10.55 billion. In their proposal, parents would pay about 20 per cent of the cost, on a sliding scale according to their means, in recognition of the gains that accrue to them directly.[4]

Early childhood education would be of greatest benefit to disadvantaged children and would help to reduce social inequality. A head start for the children of low-income families would reduce or eliminate the disadvantages they have in the education system and the resulting poor outcomes they have when they go out into the labour market or attempt to qualify for postsecondary studies.

In the 1990s two Canadian federal governments came close to introducing a plan to support day-care systems nation-wide, and then backed away. In the case of Ontario, the NDP government that set up the Royal Commission on Learning rejected out of hand its proposals for early childhood education as being too expensive. The problem is that the costs come immediately, while the benefits accrue only over time.

A large middle-class constituency of support does exist for this idea, which can also be defended in business circles as a long-term contribution to the skills and abilities of the workforce.

><><

Another approach that could help to build social solidarity is the redistribution of working time, but how this area might be approached is critical. Attempts to redistribute work within industries or unions or in the workforce generally could easily undermine social solidarity if they pit groups against one another. The only viable method, it seems to me, is to approach the idea as a long-term strategy that will gradually change how working time is distributed over a person's life cycle.

Redistribution of work can be viewed as an alternative to economic growth. It can be argued that growth is not the answer to the problem of structural unemployment and underemployment. The economy has grown by several times in the past five decades, but unemployment and underemployment persist and indeed have increased with each turn of the business cycle since the late 1960s.[5] Another line of argument arises from studies in Canada that show that much of the growing gap in earnings between younger and older workers arises from differences in the hours worked per week, not only from differences in hourly earnings.[6] At the same time, about one-third of working Canadians would prefer to work less time, while a third would prefer to work more.[7] Those working more than they want could be creating value in other ways, by giving more attention to their families, friends, and communities. Those working too little, especially underemployed and unemployed youth, could step in to fill their positions, increase their incomes, and get a start on their career paths.

Although redistribution of working time as a labour-market policy has never been given the serious consideration it has received in some European countries, it has advocates in Canada.[8] There are many straightforward ways of reducing work time: shorter workdays and workweeks, longer vacations, job sharing, education and parental leave, and early retirement, for instance. But the question of redistributing work from one group to another is a more difficult problem. Most work-sharing experiments in Canada have been designed to avoid lay-offs rather than to expand employment and are not of particular benefit to youth or other labour-market outsiders trying to get in. Most of the experiments take place in industries in which employment levels are declining and are intended to preserve the interests of existing core workers, the insiders, rather than to expand opportunities for the outsiders.

A more interesting approach from the point of view of young workers could be to examine ways of redistributing work more appropriately among the different age groups across the whole life cycle. Young people could benefit from a more gradual transition from school to work in which classroom learning is combined with workplace training and experience through arrangements such as co-operative education programs and youth apprenticeships. Once they reach their early to mid-twenties, however, youth understandably want to invest their time and energies in full-time career-path jobs that provide them with decent incomes and opportunities to develop their talents. Then, at intervals through the prime of life, they might want to take time away from a career job to learn new skills, to apply skills in different settings, or to attend to children or aging parents. After passing through the prime of life, older workers may want to phase in their retirements gradually, rather than end their careers abruptly. Some may want to continue to work and make a contribution beyond the traditional retirement age of sixty-five, but on a reduced basis, blending income from work with pension income.

Governments could introduce several measures to facilitate these kinds of life-cycle changes. They could promote the ability of prime-age workers to take extended leaves of absence for purposes of attending to their families or education. They could do this, for example, through regulations establishing the right of workers to unpaid leave, tax shelters that facilitate saving for education and training leave, legislating a right to parental leave for both sexes and supporting it through tax provisions and employment insurance, and supporting such leaves in their own employment practices. Governments could also promote the practice of voluntary phased-in retirement by making appropriate changes to the Canada Pension Plan and old age security and through their own practice as public-sector employers.[9] In the 1998 federal budget, the government did introduce the right to use RRSPs for education leave and encouraged saving for this purpose.

The cost of these measures to governments in tax benefits and pension payments could be higher than is politically acceptable, but if all age groups and classes are seen to benefit from them, they could win broad popular support.

>∞<

Alternative approaches to job creation could be of benefit to unemployed youth from low-income and middle-income families. It is not necessary for young people to be unemployed. Good public policies can ensure that any young person who wants to be can either be in an education or training program or be working. It is not unreasonable for governments to make this a condition of social assistance. If young people cannot find work on their own, a state agency should find work for them. This principle has already been accepted, it seems to me, by governments that have established compulsory workfare programs. These governments acknowledge that the cost of workfare programs exceeds the cost of passive social assistance. If they were to drop the moralizing about the work ethic and ensure that everyone placed in a job received at least the minimum wage, we could transform workfare into a positive alternative program.

Job creation does not have to mean direct employment by governments, nor do governments need to bear all of the costs. One approach, for example, is the promotion of socially useful production through third-sector or non-profit enterprises, which can produce a range of valuable goods and services with appropriate levels of government support. This support may include some degree of government subsidy — directly as one revenue stream or indirectly through favourable procurement policies — and through other forms of in-kind support. At the same time, part of the enterprises' earnings can come from their markets — that is, from other direct customers. These enterprises are ideal for situations in which there is some demand but not a sufficient market to justify the existence of a private-sector firm. A limitless range of socially useful activities exist that might not otherwise be undertaken by either the private or the public sector — for example, producing furniture for people on social assistance, organizing support for elderly people of limited means to go shopping or to maintain their homes, painting and maintaining public housing, environmental improvement of all kinds, or producing drama, music, and visual arts in areas that are now culturally isolated. Plenty of scope exists for third-sector enterprises that produce real value and are not merely a dumping ground for people who could not be employed elsewhere. They could provide useful on-the-job training to young people, especially if a conscious effort were made to focus on skills relevant to growth sectors in the economy. They could also be locations for young people to display and develop their managerial and entrepreneurial skills, an alternative to the dehumanizing production-line methods of organizing work in many of the low-wage service jobs. When the savings from reduced social assistance benefits and from payments by the end-users are taken into consideration, the net cost to governments could be negligible.[10]

These programs could take up the slack in times of high unemployment, and to avoid competition with private and public sector employers they could be gradually reduced as demand for labour increases.

><

In recent years governments, federal or provincial, have made very little movement to legislate better labour standards for the bottom layer of jobs, in which youth are overrepresented. Non-standard and contingent forms of work have few if any rights, opportunities, or benefits attached to them. Full-time, permanent jobs are much more likely to provide access to such non-wage benefits as pensions and health, dental, and other benefits. They are more likely to be unionized and protected by collective agreements with terms respecting layoffs, dismissals, and opportunities for training and advancement. Workers in non-standard jobs are also more likely to have difficulty gaining access to some of the rights and benefits assumed to come with any job, such as protection under employment standards legislation regarding health and safety, hours of work and wages, or access to employment insurance and Canada/Quebec Pension Plan benefits.

Government protection in the labour market is another type of public good that should be made available to all citizens. If they choose to do so, governments could take steps to protect young workers in these jobs and make it easier for them to organize. At a minimum, they could prohibit the worst forms of exploitation, especially for part-time and contract workers and those outside a normal workplace. Such workers should receive prorated benefits, have access to collective bargaining rights, and receive at least the minimum hourly wage and other workplace-related benefits. The benefits of collective bargaining can be extended to contingent workers in various ways. In Quebec, for example, the terms of collective agreements on wages and hours of work may be extended to all employers in a designated sector or region. Another approach would be to adopt a multi-employer certification process to get around the need to organize in each and every McDonald's franchise or Wal-Mart location, for example.

A new momentum in labour organizing has been building in workplaces in which young people are overrepresented. This initiative is the result of activism on the part of young people and the support of a growing number of Canadian unions. The labour movement is increasingly aware that it must give greater attention to this segment of the labour market if it is to be a force for social progress in Canada. By organizing themselves, in workplaces and beyond, young people can take the initiative in building social solidarity in Canada. In doing so, they will be contributing to the transformation of the labour market from a place you enter at your own risk to a source of security for all.

Notes

1 "It Has Galvanized Everybody . . ."

1 Edward Greenspon, "Cabinet Poses Policy Puzzle," *The Globe and Mail*, June 4, 1997, p.A1.
2 David Foot, *Boom, Bust, and Echo: How to Profit from the Coming Demographic Shift* (Toronto: Macfarlane Walter and Ross, 1996), p.3.
3 David Foot and J.C. Li, "Youth Unemployment in Canada: A Misplaced Priority," *Canadian Public Policy* 12,3 (1986), pp.499-506.
4 *Maclean's*, Dec. 25, 1995, p.24.
5 Cited in Angus Reid, *Shakedown: How the New Economy Is Changing Our Lives* (Toronto: Doubleday, 1996), p.87.
6 For a theoretical perspective on coming of age as a "status passage" from dependence to adult independence, see Walter R. Heinz, "Status Passages, Social Risks and the Life Course: A Conceptual Framework," in *Theoretical Advances in Life Course Research*, ed. Walter R. Heinz (Weinheim, Ger.: Deutscher Studien Verlag, 1991), pp.9-22.
7 Ulrich Beck, *Risk Society: Towards a New Modernity* (London: Sage, 1992); Anthony Giddens, *Beyond Left and Right: The Future of Radical Politics* (Stanford, Cal.: Stanford University Press, 1994); and Ulrich Beck, Anthony Giddens, and Scott Lash, *Reflexive Modernization: Politics, Tradition and Aesthetics in the Modern Social Order* (Stanford, Cal.: Stanford University Press, 1994).
8 See Jane Gaskell, *Gender Matters from School to Work* (Toronto: OISE Press, 1992).
9 For examples, see the profiles of young people in "100 Canadians to Watch," *Maclean's*, July 1, 1997. The lead story is a profile of a young woman who was the daughter of two deaf parents; despite being abandoned at age thirteen by her mother, she graduated from high school at age sixteen and won admission to Oxford University, where she became captain of the women's ice hockey team.
10 Barbara Ehrenreich, *The Hearts of Men* (New York: Anchor Press, 1983).

2 Coming of Age in Canada: 1850-1945

1 See Ronald R. Rindfuss, C. Gray Swicewood, and Rachel A. Rosenfeld, "Disorder in the Life Course: How Common and Does It Matter?" *American Sociological Review* 52 (December 1987), pp.785-801; also John Modell, Frank R. Furstenberg, Jr., and Theodore Hershberg, "Social Change and Transitions to Adulthood in Historical Perspective," *Journal of Family History* 1,1 (1976), pp.7-32.

2 I am grateful to Craig Heron for his help in clarifying this periodization. See his articles: "Factory Workers," in *Labouring Lives: Work and Workers in Nineteenth-Century Ontario*, ed. Paul Craven (Toronto: University of Toronto Press, 1995), pp.479-594; and "The Second Industrial Revolution in Canada, 1890-1930," in *Class, Community, and the Labour Movement: Wales and Canada, 1850-1930*, ed. D.R. Hopkin and G.S. Kealey (Aberystwyth: Llafur and Committee on Canadian Labour History, 1989), pp.48-66.

3 Of course, many other institutions have impinged on the lives of youth and the coming of age: religious institutions, the banking system, the labour movement, and the media, to name a few. For the purposes of a brief historical sketch, however, the four mentioned seem to be the most important.

4 See Paul Axelrod, *The Promise of Schooling: Education in Canada, 1800-1914* (Toronto: University of Toronto Press, 1997), chapter 1, for a survey of education in the British North American colonies to 1850. Unlike most studies of education in Canada, this one makes a serious effort to relate the experiences of all regions.

5 Jillian Oderkirk, "Marriage in Canada: Changing Beliefs and Behaviours, 1600-1990," *Canadian Social Trends*, Statistics Canada, Catalogue 11-008E, Summer 1990.

6 Michael B. Katz, *The People of Hamilton, Canada West: Family and Class in a Mid-Nineteenth Century City* (Cambridge, Mass.: Harvard University Press, 1975).

7 Quoted by Susan Houston, "Victorian Origins of Juvenile Delinquency: A Canadian Experience," in *Education and Social Change: Themes from Ontario's Past*, ed. Michael Katz and Paul Mattingly (New York: New York University Press, 1975), p.86.

8 Bettina Bradbury, *Working Families: Age, Gender, and Daily Survival in Industrializing Montreal* (Toronto: Oxford University Press, 1993), pp.65-66; see also pp.109-17 and chapter 4.

9 Ibid., chapter 3.

10 Heron, "Factory Workers," p.525.

11 Egerton Ryerson, "Report on a System of Public Elementary Instruction," in *Documentary History of Education in Upper Canada*, vol. IV, ed. J. George Hodgins (Toronto: Warwick and Rutler, 1897), pp.142-63.

12 See C.E. Phillips, *The Development of Education in Canada* (Toronto: Gage, 1957).

13 Alison Prentice, *The School Promoters: Education and Social Class in Mid-Nineteenth Century Upper Canada* (Toronto: McClelland and Stewart, 1977); see also Houston, "Victorian Origins of Juvenile Delinquency."

14 Bruce Curtis, *Building the Educational State: Canada West, 1836-1871* (London, Ont.: The Althouse Press, 1988).

15 Axelrod, *Promise of Schooling*, pp.32-43.

16 Ibid. There is much more detailed and nuanced interpretation to this story than I can do justice to here. For example, there was tension from the start between centralized control of education and community-based involvement — an issue that is still with us today. The struggles of different religious denominations to control the schooling of their young also runs through the history of public education to the present day; it is one strand of the "school choice" movement. Axelrod's book is a good introduction to this story.

17 Axelrod, *Promise of Schooling*, pp.70-77.

18 Prentice, *School Promoters*, pp.60-62.

19 See Axelrod, *Promise of Schooling*, pp.60-63, for a sketch of the development of secondary schools in Canada.

20 For detailed background see Craig Heron, "The Second Industrial Revolution in Canada, 1890-1930," and Heron, "The Crisis of the Craftsman: Hamilton's Metal Workers in the Early Twentieth Century," both in *The Consolidation of Capitalism:*

1896-1929, Readings in Canadian Social History, vol. 4, ed. Gregory S. Kealey and Michael S. Cross (Toronto: McClelland and Stewart, 1983), pp.77-113.

21 Harvey Krahn and Graham Lowe, *Work, Industry, and Canadian Society*, 2nd ed. (Toronto: Nelson, 1993), p.23.

22 Canada, Department of Trade and Commerce, Census and Statistics Office, *Occupations of the People*, vol. 6, *Fifth Census of Canada, 1911* (Ottawa: King's Printer, 1915), Table 1, p.3.

23 Mercedes Steedman, *Angels of the Workplace: Women and the Construction of Gender Relations in the Canadian Clothing Industry 1890-1940* (Toronto: Oxford University Press, 1997), chapter 2.

24 Steedman, *Angels of the Workplace*, p.1.

25 Quoted in Craig Heron, "The High School and the Household Economy in Working-Class Hamilton, 1890-1940," *Historical Studies in Education* 7,2 (Fall 1995), p.241.

26 This Commission was noteworthy for being the first of many uses of royal commissions by future Prime Minister William Lyon Mackenzie King, then the youthful federal labour minister. See Jamie Swift's description of the Commission in *Wheel of Fortune: Work and Life in the Age of Falling Expectations* (Toronto: Between the Lines, 1995), chapter 4.

27 Parliament of Canada, *Report of the Royal Commission on Industrial Training and Technical Education*, Sessional Paper no. 191d, Ottawa, 1913, p.39.

28 Ibid., p.15.

29 Ibid., pp.2084-92.

30 See Jamie Swift's description of the "High School Debate" in *Wheel of Fortune*, pp.70-72.

31 For a brief overview of this literature, see Rebecca Coulter and Ivor Goodson, "Introduction," in *Rethinking Vocationalism: Whose Work/Life Is It?* ed. Rebecca Coulter and Ivor Goodson (Toronto: Our Schools/Our Selves, 1993); see also Axelrod, *Promise of Schooling*, pp.110-13; and Swift, *Wheel of Fortune*, chapter 4.

32 See Coulter and Goodson, "Introduction," p.2, and Jane Gaskell, "Constructing Vocationalism: Barbara, Darlene and Me," pp.52-68, both in *Rethinking Vocationalism*, ed. Coulter and Goodson; see also Nancy Jackson and Jane Gaskell, "White Collar Vocationalism: The Rise of Commercial Education in Ontario and British Columbia, 1870-1920," *Curriculum Inquiry* 17 (1987); and Gaskell, *Gender Matters*.

33 Parliament of Canada, *Report of the Royal Commission on Industrial Training and Technical Education*, p.18.

34 See Axelrod, *Promise of Schooling*, pp.110-13.

35 See Christopher Anstead and Ivor Goodson, "Structuring and Restructuring Vocational Knowledge: The Commercial Curriculum at the London Technical and Commercial High School, 1920-1940," in *Rethinking Vocationalism*, ed. Coulter and Goodson, pp.28-51.

36 Gaskell, "Constructing Vocationalism," pp.52-68.

37 Heron, "High School and the Household Economy."

38 Oderkirk, "Marriage in Canada."

39 Statistics from James Struthers, "Great Depression," *The Canadian Encyclopedia*, 1st ed. (Edmonton: Hurtig, 1985), p.770.

40 Victor Howard, "Unemployment Relief Camps," *Canadian Encyclopedia*, p.1866.

41 Rebecca Prieger Coulter, "Managing Youth Unemployment: The Dominion-Provincial Youth Training Programme, 1937-1940," *Journal of Education Administration and Foundations* 8,2 (1993), pp.39-53.

42 The report to the Anglican bishops is described in Coulter, "Managing Youth Unemployment."

43 H.A. Weir, "Unemployed Youth," in *Canada's Unemployment Problem*, ed. L. Richter (Toronto: Macmillan, 1939), pp.147-48.

44 Struthers, "Great Depression."

45 Coulter, "Managing Youth Unemployment," p.40.

46 Rebecca Prieger Coulter, "Schooling, Work and Life: Reflections of the Young in the 1940s," in *Rethinking Vocationalism*, pp.69-86.

47 Oderkirk, "Marriage in Canada."
48 Karl Polanyi, *The Great Transformation* (Boston: Beacon Press, 1944).
49 Ibid., p.73.

3 From Golden Age to Risk Society: The Postwar World

1 I have relied on a number of sources for accounts of the postwar evolution of social and labour-market policy: A.W. Johnson, "Social Policy in Canada: The Past as It Conditions the Present," in *The Future of Social Welfare Systems in Canada and the United Kingdom*, ed. Shirley B. Seward (Halifax: Institute for Research on Public Policy, 1987); Isabella Bakker and Katherine Scott, "From the Postwar to the Post-Liberal Keynesian Welfare State," in *Understanding Canada: Building on the New Canadian Political Economy*, ed. Wallace Clement (Kingston and Montreal: McGill-Queen's University Press, 1997); Stephen McBride and John Shields, *Dismantling a Nation: The Transition to Corporate Rule in Canada*, 2nd ed. (Halifax: Fernwood Publishing, 1997); John Myles, "When Markets Fail: Social Welfare in Canada and the United States," in *Welfare States in Transition: National Adaptations in Global Economies*, ed. Gosta Esping-Andersen (London: Sage, 1996), pp.116-40.

2 See especially Canadian Youth Commission, *Youth and Jobs in Canada* (Toronto: Ryerson Press, 1945) and Canadian Youth Commission, *Youth Challenges the Educators* (Toronto: Ryerson Press, 1946), as well as the report on the Canadian Youth Commission in Coulter, "Schooling, Work and Life," pp.69-86.

3 V.C. Fowke, "The National Policy — Old and New," in *Approaches to Canadian Economic History*, ed. W.T. Easterbrook and M.H. Watkins (Toronto: McClelland and Stewart, 1967).

4 Gosta Esping-Andersen, *The Three Worlds of Welfare Capitalism* (Princeton, N.J.: Princeton University Press, 1990).

5 The distinction between the primary and secondary labour markets is based on dual labour-market theory. For a good overview of theories of the labour market, and particularly of labour-market segmentation, see Harvey Krahn and Graham Lowe, *Work, Industry, and Canadian Society*, 3rd ed. (Scarborough, Ont.: Nelson Canada, 1998), chapter 3.

6 The pattern for young working-class males that I am describing here is adapted from Paul Osterman's observations of young men in a large U.S. city in *Getting Started: The Youth Labour Market* (Cambridge Mass.: MIT Press, 1980).

7 Frank Levy, *Dollars and Dreams: The Changing American Income Distribution* (New York: W.W. Norton, 1988), pp.78-82, cited in Myles, "When Markets Fail," p.120. For Canadian evidence, see John Myles, Garnett Picot, and Ted Wannell, "Does Postindustrialism Matter? The Canadian Experience," in *Changing Classes: Stratification and Mobility in Post-industrial Societies* (London: Sage, 1993), pp.171-94.

8 Jane Gaskell, "Introduction," in *Transitions: Schooling and Employment in Canada*, ed. Paul Anisef and Paul Axelrod (Toronto: Thompson Educational Publishing, 1993), pp.xii.

9 Ibid.

10 For the main arguments of "human capital theory," see Gary Becker, *Human Capital: A Theoretical and Empirical Analysis with Special Reference to Education*, 2nd ed. (New York: National Bureau of Economic Research, 1975).

11 William H. Whyte, *The Organization Man* (New York: Simon, 1956).

12 Paul Goodman, *Growing up Absurd* (New York: Vintage, 1960), pp.17, 34-35.

13 Erik Erikson, *Identity: Youth and Crisis* (New York: Norton, 1968). James Côté and Anton Allahar, *Generation on Hold: Coming of Age in the Late Twentieth Century* (Toronto: Stoddart, 1994), contains an interesting discussion of Erikson's theory of the moratorium and its relevance to youth in the 1990s. See chapter 6 for a discussion of Côté and Allahar's thesis.

14 Economists debate the causes of this crisis and the relative importance of various factors. Some of them argue that the system of mass production by well-paid, semi-skilled

workers in large-scale manufacturing enterprises like the auto industry had run its course, that no significant additional productivity gains could be made with the labour process of scientific management. This view is developed by Peter Drucker in his book *Post-Capitalist Society* (New York: HarperCollins, 1993). It is also central to the theory of the French regulation school of economists; the most accessible account is by Alain Lipietz, *Towards a New Economic Order: Postfordism, Ecology, and Democracy* (New York: Oxford University Press, 1992).

15 Cy Gonick, *The Great Economic Debate* (Toronto: Lorimer, 1987), pp.341-42; see also S.H. Heap, "World Profitability Crisis in the 1970s: Some Empirical Evidence," *Capital and Class* 12 (1980/81); and James O'Connor, *Accumulation Crisis* (Oxford: Basil Blackwell, 1986).

16 Klaus Schwab and Claus Smadja, "Power and Policy: The New Economic World Order," *Harvard Business Review*, November-December 1994.

17 Peter F. Drucker, "The Changed World Economy," *Foreign Affairs*, Spring 1986.

18 Economic Council of Canada, *Good Jobs, Bad Jobs: Employment in the Service Economy* (Ottawa: Department of Supply and Services, 1990). See also the longer accompanying analysis done by the Economic Council of Canada, *Employment in the Service Economy* (Ottawa: Department of Supply and Services, 1991).

19 Human Resources Development Canada, *Improving Social Security in Canada* (Ottawa: HRDC, 1994), p.16.

20 See Gordon Betcherman, Norm Leckie, Kathryn McMullen, and Christina Caron, *The Canadian Workplace in Transition* (Kingston, Ont.: Queen's University Industrial Relations Centre Press, 1994).

21 In North America this ideology is often called "neo-conservatism" while in the rest of the world it is called "neo-liberalism," reflecting its roots in the nineteenth-century liberal doctrine of laissez-faire. See the discussion of this point in McBride and Shields, *Dismantling a Nation*, pp.17-34. Here I will adopt McBride and Shields's usage, referring to free-market ideology as neo-liberalism and reserving the use of neo-conservatism for conservatism in social policy.

22 Employment and Immigration Canada, *Labour Market Development in the 1980s* (The Dodge Report) (Ottawa: Minister of Supply and Services, 1981).

23 Harvey Krahn and Graham Lowe, "Young Workers in the Service Economy," Working Paper 90-14, Economic Council of Canada, Ottawa, 1990.

24 Deborah Sunter, "Youths — Waiting It Out," *Perspectives on Labour and Income*, Statistics Canada, Catalogue 75-001E, Spring 1994.

25 See Lindsay Redpath, "Education and Job Mismatch among Canadian University Graduates: Implications for Employers," *The Canadian Journal of Higher Education* 24,2 (1994), pp.89-114.

26 Krahn and Lowe, "Young Workers in the Service Economy," p.43.

27 Oderkirk, "Marriage in Canada."

28 Statistics Canada, *The Daily*, Oct. 14, 1997 (http://www.statcan.ca/english/search/daily.htm).

29 Statistics Canada, *The Daily*, Oct. 14, 1997.

4 Education and Changing Aspirations

1 Quoted in Jane Gaskell, *Secondary Schools in Canada: The National Report of the Exemplary Schools Project* (Toronto: Canadian Education Association, 1995), p.56.

2 "Rockland" is described in Lars Osberg, Fred Wien, and Jan Grude, *Vanishing Jobs: Canada's Changing Workplaces* (Toronto: Lorimer, 1995), chapter 6.

3 The completion rates are from Statistics Canada's School Leavers Follow-up Survey. The results of this 1995 survey are reported in Jeff Frank, *After High School: The First Years: The First Report of the School Leavers Follow-up Survey, 1995* (Ottawa: Human Resources Development Canada and Statistics Canada, 1996). For statistics on high-school completion and postsecondary studies by gender, see Frank, *After High School*, also available through the Internet at http://www.hrdc-drhc.gc.ca. The

participation rates are from Statistics Canada, *Education in Canada*, Catalogue no. 81-229; and Organization for Economic Co-operation and Development (OECD), *Education at a Glance: OECD Indicators* (Paris, 1997).

4 Statistics Canada, *Education in Canada*, Catalogue no. 81-229, various years; and OECD, *Education at a Glance*, p.172.

5 OECD, *Education at a Glance*, p.59.

6 Harvey Krahn and Graham Lowe, "Transitions to Work: Findings from a Longitudinal Study of High-school and University Graduates in Three Canadian Cities," in *Making Their Way: Education, Training, and the Labour Market in Canada and Britain*, ed. David Ashton and Graham Lowe (Toronto: University of Toronto Press, 1991), pp.134-37.

7 Susan Empson-Warner and Harvey Krahn, "Unemployment and Occupational Aspirations: A Panel Study of High School Graduates," *Canadian Review of Sociology and Anthropology* 29,1 (1992), pp.38-54.

8 See Krahn and Lowe, "Transitions to Work."

9 E. Dianne Looker, "Interconnected Transitions and Their Costs: Gender and Urban/Rural Differences in the Transitions to Work," in *Transitions*, ed. Anisef and Axelrod.

10 Steven Theobald, "Harder for Them to Make Ends Meet, Survey Shows," *The Toronto Star*, Aug. 27, 1997, p.A1.

11 See Charles Jones, Lorna Marsden, and Lorne Tepperman, *Lives of Their Own: The Individualization of Women's Lives* (Toronto: Oxford University Press, 1990), for a good discussion of the forces impelling women into the labour force.

12 Conference Board of Canada, *Dropping Out: The Cost to Canada* (Ottawa: Conference Board of Canada, 1992).

13 See, for example, Economic Council of Canada, *A Lot to Learn: Education and Training in Canada* (Ottawa: Department of Supply and Services, 1992); Ontario Premier's Council, *People and Skills in the New Global Economy* (Toronto: Queen's Printer for Ontario, 1990); and Michael E. Porter, *Canada at the Crossroads: The Reality of a New Competitive Environment* (Ottawa: Business Council on National Issues and the Government of Canada, 1991).

14 This is the estimate made by Statistics Canada on the basis of its School Leavers Survey of 1991 and the School Leavers Follow-up Survey of 1995. (See note 3, chapter 4.) Results of the 1991 survey are reported in Sid Gilbert et al., *Leaving School: Results from a National Survey Comparing School Leavers and High School Graduates 18 to 20 Years of Age* (Ottawa: Statistics Canada and Human Resources and Labour Canada, 1993).

15 A recent work, which summarizes the findings of earlier studies in its first chapter, is Julian Tanner, Harvey Krahn, and Timothy F. Hartnagel, *Fractured Transitions from School to Work: Revisiting the Dropout Problem* (Toronto: Oxford University Press, 1995). Other key works are Gilbert et al., *Leaving School*; George Radwanski, *Ontario Study of the Relevance of Education and the Issue of Dropouts* (Toronto: Ontario Ministry of Education, 1987); W.H. Spain and D.B. Sharpe, *The Early School Leavers: Initial Survey* (St. John's, Nfld.: Centre for Educational Research and Development, Memorial University of Newfoundland, 1990); W.H. Spain, D.B. Sharpe, and Andrea Mundle, *Life after School: A Profile of Early Leavers in Newfoundland* (St. John's, Nfld.: Centre for Educational Research and Development, Memorial University of Newfoundland, 1991). The most recent basic statistics on dropping out are found in Frank, *After High School*.

16 Frank, *After High School*.

17 Gilbert et al., *Leaving School*, p.23.

18 Tanner et al. *Fractured Transitions from School to Work*, p.22.

19 Sandro Contenta, *Rituals of Failure: What Schools Really Teach* (Toronto: Between the Lines, 1993), p.31.

20 Paul Willis, *Learning to Labour: How Working Class Kids Get Working Class Jobs* (New York: Columbia University Press, 1977).

21 Julian Tanner, "Reluctant Rebels: A Case Study of Edmonton High-School Dropouts," in *Making Their Way*, ed. Ashton and Lowe.

22 Frank, *After High School*.

23 See Paul Anisef, G. Paasche, and A.H. Turrittin, *Is the Die Cast? Educational Achievements and Work Destinations of Ontario Youth* (Toronto: Ontario Ministry of Colleges and Universities, 1980); John Porter, Marion Porter, and B.R. Blishen, *Stations and Callings: Making It Through the School System* (Toronto: Methuen, 1982); and Dianne Looker and Peter Pineo, "Social Psychological Variables and Their Relevance to the Status Attainment of Teenagers," *American Journal of Sociology* 88,6 (1983), pp.1195-1219.

24 For a description of the study, see Lesley Andres Bellamy, "Life Trajectories, Action, and Negotiating the Transition from High School," in *Transitions*, ed. Anisef and Axelrod. For more on Pierre Bourdieu's ideas on social or cultural capital, see his essay "The Forms of Capital," in *Handbook of Theory and Research for the Sociology of Education*, ed. J.C. Richardson (New York: Greenwood Press, 1986), pp.241-58.

25 Alanna Mitchell, "Tuition Squeeze Not Stopping Students," *The Globe and Mail*, Sept. 30, 1997.

26 Statistics Canada, "University Tuition Fees, 1997/98," *The Daily*, Aug. 25, 1997 (http://www.statcan.ca/english/search/daily.htm).

27 On this see David Ashton and Graham Lowe, "Conclusion: Towards an Explanation of Transition Patterns," in *Making Their Way*, ed. Ashton and Lowe.

28 On the "cafeteria model," see Jane Gaskell, "Education as a Preparation for Work in Canada: Structure, Policy and Student Response," in *Making Their Way*, ed. Ashton and Lowe.

29 Economic Council of Canada, *A Lot to Learn*, p.47.

30 See Christoph F. Buechtemann et al., "Roads to Work: School-to-Work Transition Paths in Germany and the United States," *Industrial Relations Journal* 24,2 (1993), pp.97-111.

31 See the major policy statements on education prepared by these organizations: International Commission on Education for the Twenty-first Century, *Learning: The Treasure Within* (Paris: UNESCO, 1996); Organization for Economic Co-operation and Development (OECD), *Lifelong Learning for All* (Paris, 1996).

32 See, for example, Thomas Schweitzer, *The State of Education in Canada* (Montreal: The Institute for Research on Public Policy, 1995), as well as Economic Council of Canada, *A Lot to Learn*.

33 See Stephen B. Lawton, *Busting Bureaucracy to Reclaim Our Schools* (Montreal: The Institute for Research on Public Policy, 1995); Andrew Nikiforuk, *School's Out: The Catastrophe in Public Education and What We Can Do about It* (Toronto: Macfarlane Walter and Ross, 1993); and Jennifer Lewington and Graham Orpwood, *Overdue Assignment: Taking Responsibility for Canada's Schools* (Rexdale, Ont.: John Wiley and Sons, 1993).

34 See the Conference Board of Canada, *Employability Skills Profile* (Ottawa, 1992).

35 For example, Peter C. Emberley and Waller R. Newell, *Bankrupt Education: The Decline of Liberal Education in Canada* (Toronto: University of Toronto Press, 1994).

36 See Contenta, *Rituals of Failure*.

37 Tom R. Williams and Holly Millinoff, *Canada's Schools: Report Card for the 1990s: A CEA Opinion Poll* (Toronto: Canadian Education Association, 1990), cited in Schweitzer, *State of Education in Canada*, pp.29-34.

38 Maude Barlow and Heather-jane Robertson, *Class Warfare: The Assault on Canada's Schools* (Toronto: Key Porter Books, 1994).

39 This claim is the first selling point offered in a two-page advertisement for the Canadian Association of Independent Schools, whose members include Upper Canada College for boys in Toronto and Miss Edgar's and Miss Cramp's school for girls in Westmount. *Maclean's*, Nov. 24, 1997, following p.62.

40 See Contenta, *Rituals of Failure*, pp.99ff.

41 See Murray Dobbin, *Charter Schools: Charting a Course to Social Division* (Ottawa: Canadian Centre for Policy Alternatives, 1997). For a more sympathetic analysis of educational choice, see Bruce W. Wilkinson, *Educational Choice: Necessary but Not Sufficient* (Montreal: Institute for Research on Public Policy, 1994).

42　Commission of Inquiry on Canadian University Education (1991), *Report on Canadian University Education* (Smith Commission Report) (Ottawa: AUCC, 1991).

43　Victor Dwyer, "Academia, Inc.," *Maclean's*, Nov. 24, 1997, pp.66-71.

44　This scenario has been projected in different versions in various places. See the series on Canadian universities in *The Globe and Mail*, Dec. 11 to 20, 1995, as well as David Bercuson, Robert Bothwell, and J.L. Granatstein, *Petrified Campus: The Crisis in Canada's Universities* (Toronto: Random House, 1997), chapter 2.

45　Edward Greenspon, "Martin Adopts Unofficial New Portfolio," *The Globe and Mail*, Oct. 16, 1997, p.A4.

5　Making Their Way: The Labour-Market Experience

1　Douglas Coupland, *Generation X: Tales of an Accelerated Culture* (New York: St. Martin's Press, 1991), p.5.

2　See Statistics Canada, *Labour Force Update: Youths and the Labour Market* (Ottawa: Statistics Canada, Spring 1997).

3　Ibid.

4　Ibid.

5　Deborah Sunter, "School, Work, and Dropping Out," *Perspectives on Labour and Income*, Statistics Canada, Catalogue No. 75-001, Summer 1993.

6　See Sunter, "Youths — Waiting It Out."

7　Statistics Canada, *Labour Force Update: Youths and the Labour Market*.

8　See Krahn and Lowe, "Transitions to Work." The reports on the National Graduates Surveys by Statistics Canada during the 1980s give a similar figure. Reports on postsecondary graduating classes in the 1990s no longer give the figures for incidence of unemployment experiences during the two years after graduation. Considering the more difficult conditions in the 1990s, we can safely assume that well over half go through periods of unemployment after graduating.

9　Statistics Canada, *Labour Force Update: Youths and the Labour Market*.

10　Michael Paju, *The Class of '90 Revisited: Report of the 1995 Follow-up Survey of 1990 Graduates* (Ottawa: Statistics Canada, 1997).

11　See ibid. for details.

12　Frank, *After High School*.

13　Don Little and Louise Lapierre, *The Class of 90: A Compendium of Findings from the 1992 National Graduates Survey of 1990 Graduates* (Ottawa: Statistics Canada, 1996), p.28.

14　Statistics Canada, *Labour Force Update: Youths and the Labour Market*.

15　See Stuart Conger, Bryan Hiebert, and Elizabeth Hong-Farrell, *Career and Employment Counselling in Canada* (Ottawa: Canadian Labour Force Development Board, 1994); Canadian Labour Force Development Board, *Putting the Pieces Together: Toward a Coherent Transition System for Canada's Labour Force*, Report of the Task Force on Transition into Employment to the Canadian Labour Force Development Board (Ottawa, 1994); as well as Organization for Economic Co-operation and Development (OECD), *Mapping the Future: Young People and Career Guidance* (Paris, 1996).

16　See C.F. Buechtemann et al., "Roads to Work: School-to-Work Transition Patterns in Germany and the United States," *Industrial Relations Journal* 24,2 (1993), pp.97-111.

17　The overview that follows of occupations of young Canadians by education level and gender is based on an analysis of the findings of Statistics Canada's School Leavers Follow-up Survey of 1995. See Richard Marquardt, "Labour Market Participation, Employment, and Unemployment," in *High School May Not Be Enough: Analysis of Results from the School Leavers' Follow-up Survey of 1995* (Ottawa: Human Resources Development Canada and Statistics Canada, 1998).

18　Paju, "Class of '90 Revisited," Table 3.4, p.16.

19　Harvey Krahn, *Quality of Work in the Service Sector*, General Social Survey Analysis Series (Ottawa: Statistics Canada, 1992).

20 Statistics Canada, *Labour Force Update: Youths and the Labour Market.*

21 Richard Marquardt, "Quality of Youth Employment," in *High School May Not Be Enough.*

22 Ibid.

23 Andrew Heisz, "Changes in Job Tenure and Job Stability in Canada," Analytical Studies Branch, no. 95 (Ottawa: Statistics Canada, 1996).

24 See, for example, William Bridges, *JobShift: How to Prosper in a Workplace without Jobs* (Menlo Park, Cal.: Addison-Wesley, 1994).

25 Marquardt, "Quality of Youth Employment."

26 Ibid.

27 John Hagan, Marie Huxter, and Patricia Parker, "Class Structure and Legal Practice: Inequality and Mobility among Toronto Lawyers," *Law and Society Review* 22,1 (1988), pp.28-55, cited in Jones, Marsden, and Tepperman, *Lives of Their Own*, p.43.

28 For a survey of youth attitudes to work in different labour-market segments, see Harvey Krahn and Graham Lowe, *Young Workers in the Service Economy*, Working Paper no. 14 (Ottawa: Economic Council of Canada, 1990).

29 Heather Menzies, *Whose Brave New World? The Information Highway and the New Economy* (Toronto: Between the Lines, 1996).

30 See Cameron Lynne Macdonald and Carmen Sirianni, "The Service Society and the Changing Experience of Work," in *Working in the Service Society*, ed. Cameron Lynne Macdonald and Carmen Sirianni (Philadelphia: Temple University Press, 1997), pp.1-26.

31 Quoted by Macdonald and Sirianni, "Service Society and the Changing Experience," p.7.

32 Ernest B. Akyeampong, "A Statistical Portrait of the Trade Union Movement," *Perspectives on Labour and Income* 9,4 (Winter 1997), pp.45-54.

33 Ted Wannell, "The Distribution of Employment by Employer Size: Recent Canadian Evidence," Analytical Studies Series no. 39 (Ottawa: Statistics Canada, 1991); René Morissette, "Canadian Jobs and Firm Size: Do Smaller Firms Pay Less?" Analytical Studies Series no. 35 (Ottawa: Statistics Canada, 1991); Garnett Picot, J. Baldwin, and R. Dupuy, "Have Small Firms Created a Disproportionate Share of New Jobs in Canada? A Reassessment of the Facts," Analytical Studies Series no. 71 (Ottawa: Statistics Canada, 1994).

34 A few accounts of recent organizing drives by young workers in Canada can be found in: Naomi Klein, "Salesgirl Solidarity," *This Magazine*, February 1995; Clive Thompson, "State of the Union," *The Globe and Mail Report on Business Magazine*, April 1998, pp.72-82; and several articles in *Our Times* 14,3 (July 1995) and *Our Times* 17,4 (July/August 1998).

35 Harvey Krahn, "On the Permanence of Human Capital: Use It or Lose It," *Policy Options*, July/August 1997, pp.16-19; see also Karen Kelly, Linda Howatson-Leo, and Warren Clark, "I Feel Overqualified for My Job . . ." *Canadian Social Trends*, Winter 1997, pp.11-15.

36 Human Resources Development Canada, *Canadian Occupational Projection System: 1998 Macroeconomic Reference Scenario* (Ottawa, 1998).

37 Wayne Roth, *Canadian Occupational Projection System: A Presentation of Results Using a Revised Framework*, rev. ed. (Ottawa: Human Resources Development Canada, 1998, p.7).

38 Frank, *After High School.*

6 Changing Patterns: Earnings, Incomes, and Personal Life

1 Derek Holt, "Will the Future Remain Bleak for Today's Youths?" *Policy Options* 19,3 (April 1998), p.18.

2 See Charles Beach and George A. Slotsve, *Are We Becoming Two Societies? Income Polarization and the Myth of the Declining Middle Class in Canada* (Toronto: C.D. Howe Institute, 1996). There is a much larger discussion about what is happening to

tax rates and social transfers and their implications for inequality in Canada, but that is not the focus here.

The distinction between polarization and inequality can be confusing. It is not complicated. Beach and Slotsve define middle-class earners as those making between 25 per cent and 175 per cent of the median annual wage. The median is the wage level that divides the working population in half; 50 per cent earn more than this, 50 per cent earn less. When the median declines, as it has done, the average income of all those who earn between 25 per cent and 175 per cent of the median can decline without changing the size of the middle class. Beach and Slotsve found that the average earnings of those earning less than 25 per cent of the median declined, as did the average earnings of those earning between 25 per cent and 175 per cent of the median, but the average earnings of those earning over 175 per cent of the median increased. The result was greater inequality but not greater polarization.

3 A word of warning: different studies use different data bases, different time periods, and different methods for analysing trends. They also measure different things. For example, some examine the annual earnings of full-time, full-year workers; others look at weekly or hourly wages; while still others may include total income from all sources. I do not intend to lay out all of this detail on methods here. I will identify the sources, and readers who are interested can look into these studies on their own.

4 The figures are from Gordon Betcherman and Norm Leckie, *Youth Employment and Education Trends in the 1980s and 1990s* (Ottawa: Canadian Policy Research Networks, 1997). See also René Morissette, John Myles, and Garnett Picot, "What Is Happening to Earnings Inequality in Canada?" Research Paper no. 60, Analytical Studies Branch, Statistics Canada, Ottawa, 1993, as well as, by the same authors, "Earnings Inequality and the Distribution of Working Time in Canada," *Canadian Business Economics* 2,3 (Spring 1994).

5 Paul Beaudry and David Green, *Cohort Patterns in Canadian Earnings: Assessing the Role of Skill Premia in Inequality Trends*, The Canadian Institute for Advanced Research Program in Economic Growth and Policy, Working Paper no. 96, 1997. The authors analysed the earning patterns of seven different cohorts of Canadian workers — that is, those groups that reached the age of twenty-five or twenty-six in 1964, 1968, 1972, 1978, 1982, 1986, and 1990. The researchers tracked the average weekly earnings of each group as far as possible from the age of twenty-five to twenty-six up to 1993. They tracked the first group to the age of fifty-four, the second group to the age of fifty, the third to forty-six, and so on. The data on earnings are adjusted to eliminate the short-term effects of fluctuations in the business cycle affecting different cohorts at different ages. This provides a clearer picture of long-term trends. Each cohort is divided into men and women, as well as those with a university education and those with only a high school diploma or less.

6 For another study with slightly different findings but the same general patterns, see Susan Crompton, "Employment Prospects for High School Graduates," *Perspectives on Labour and Income* 7,3 (Autumn 1995), pp.8-13. Crompton does not adjust her data to compensate for different points in the business cycle. She examines four cohorts of twenty-five- to twenty-nine-year-olds from 1979 to 1993. She also finds that the gender earnings gap is closing among university graduates, but only slightly or not at all among those with only a high-school education. There has been a steady decline in the real annual earnings of both male and female high-school graduates with each successive cohort. There has also been a steady decline in the earnings of male university graduates in this age group, but slight increases for the female university graduates.

7 Steven Davis, "Cross-Country Patterns of Change in Relative Wages," National Bureau of Economic Research Working Paper no. 4085, 1993, cited in Morissette, Myles, and Picot, "Earnings Inequality and the Distribution of Working Time."

8 R.B. Freeman and K. Needels, "Skill Differentials in Canada in an Era of Rising Labor Market Inequality," National Bureau of Economic Research Working Paper no. 3826, 1991, cited in René Morissette, "Why Has Inequality in Weekly Earnings Increased in Canada?" Research Paper no. 80, Analytical Studies Branch, Statistics Canada, Ottawa, 1995.

9 Gordon Betcherman and René Morissette, "Recent Youth Labour Market Experiences in Canada," Research Paper no. 63, Analytical Studies Branch, Statistics Canada, Ottawa, 1994.

10 For the workforce as a whole, some of the increase in inequality of earnings is explained by shifts of industry and union status, but these are not the main factors; see Morissette, "Why Has Inequality in Weekly Earnings Increased?" p.21.

11 For details see Morissette, Myles, and Picot, "What Is Happening to Earnings Inequality?" and Morissette, Myles, and Picot, "Earnings Inequality and the Distribution of Working Time." See also Morissette, "Why Has Inequality in Weekly Earnings Increased?"

12 Garnett Picot, "Working Time, Wages and Earnings Inequality in Canada, 1981-1993," Statistics Canada, Business and Labour Market Analysis Division, Ottawa, 1996, p.16.

13 For the summary of possible explanations that follows, I am indebted primarily to Morissette, "Why Has Inequality in Weekly Earnings Increased?"

14 Freeman and Needels, "Skill Differentials in Canada."

15 See John Myles, "Is There a Post-Fordist Life Course?" in *Institutions and Gate-Keeping in the Life Course*, ed. Walter R. Heinz (Weinheim, Ger.: Deutscher Studien Verlag, 1992), pp.171-85.

16 Statistics Canada, *Income Distributions by Size in Canada, 1996*, Catalogue no. 13-207-XPB, Ottawa, December 1997, Table 66, pp.180-81.

17 John Crupi, "Squeezing out Squeegee Kids," *The Ottawa X Press*, July 1, 1998, p.9.

18 On moral panics see Stanley Cohen, *Folk Devils and Moral Panics: The Creation of the Mods and Rockers*, 2nd ed. (New York: St Martin's Press, 1980); Stuart Hall, Chas Critcher, Tony Jefferson, John Clarke, and Brian Roberts *Policing the Crisis: Mugging, the State, and Law and Order* (London: Macmillan, 1978). For discussion of moral panics affecting Canadian youth, see Julian Tanner, Graham Lowe, and Harvey Krahn, "Youth Unemployment and Moral Panics," *Perception* 7,5 (1984), pp.27-29; Tanner, Krahn, and Hartnagel, *Fractured Transitions*; as well as Bernard Schissel, *Blaming Children: Youth Crime, Moral Panics and the Politics of Hate* (Halifax: Fernwood Publishing, 1997).

19 Marlene Webber, *Street Kids: The Tragedy of Canada's Runaways* (Toronto: University of Toronto Press, 1991), p.248.

20 Monica Boyd and Doug Norris, "Leaving the Nest: The Impact of Family Structure," *Canadian Social Trends*, Autumn 1995, pp.14-17.

21 See Boyd and Norris, "Leaving the Nest"; and Barbara Mitchell and Ellen Gee, "Young Adults Returning Home: Implications for Social Policy," in *Youth in Transition: Perspectives on Research and Policy* (Toronto: Thompson Educational Publishing, 1996), pp.61-71.

22 Côté and Allahar, *Generation on Hold*.

23 See Tanner, Lowe, and Krahn, "Youth Unemployment and Moral Panics"; Sharon Kirsh, *Unemployment: Its Impact on Body and Soul* (Toronto: Canadian Mental Health Association, 1983); and John N. Lavis and Mark Farrant, "Unemployment, Job Insecurity, and Health: From Understanding to Action," Health Canada, Ottawa, 1998.

24 Statistics Canada, *Causes of Death*, Catalogue no. 84-208-XPB (prior to 1990, Catalogue no. 84-203), Ottawa, various years. For mortality rates 1993-95, see Statistics Canada, *Mortality: Summary List of Causes*, Catalogue no. 84-209-XPB, Ottawa, 1993, 1994, and 1995.

25 Boyd and Norris, "Leaving the Nest."

26 John Z. Zhao, Fernando Rajulton, and Zenaida R. Ravanera, "Leaving Parental Homes in Canada: Effects of Family Structure, Gender, and Culture," *Canadian Journal of Sociology* 20,1 (1995), pp.31-50.

27 See Karen Hughes, "Women in Non-traditional Occupations," *Perspectives on Labour and Income*, 7,3 (Autumn 1995), pp.14-19.

28 Robert Matas, "Women Earning 52% of What Men Make, New Study Finds," *The Globe and Mail*, March 2, 1998.

29 Jones, Marsden, and Tepperman, *Lives of Their Own.*
30 Statistics Canada, "Report on the Demographic Situation in Canada," *The Daily*, March 25, 1997.
31 Steven Taylor, "Love, Work and the Bottom Line," *The Globe and Mail*, Feb. 7, 1995. A more scientific measure shows that the education levels of spouses are strongly correlated. Although Steven Taylor's case may be an exception, we can take education level as a reasonable proxy for income level among people of the same age. See Table 9 in M.L. Blackburn and D.E. Bloom, "The Distribution of Family Income: Measuring and Explaining Changes in the 1980s for Canada and the United States," in *Small Differences That Matter: Labor Markets and Income Maintenance in Canada and the United States*, ed. D. Card (Chicago: University of Chicago Press for the National Bureau of Economic Research, 1993).
32 Statistics Canada, *Income Distributions by Size in Canada*, Ottawa, 1997; see also Alanna Mitchell, "Gap Grows between Rich and Poor," *The Globe and Mail*, Dec. 23, 1997, p.A1.

7 Policy Responses to Labour-Market Problems

1 Organization for Economic Co-operation and Development (OECD), *The OECD Jobs Study: Facts, Analysis, Strategies* (Paris, 1994), p.44.
2 Ibid., p.45.
3 Esping-Andersen, *Three Worlds of Welfare Capitalism.*
4 Here are a few of them: British Columbia, *A Legacy for Learners*, Report of the Royal Commission on Education (Vancouver: Province of British Columbia, 1988); Ontario Premier's Council, *People and Skills in the New Global Economy*; Michael Bloom, *Reaching for Success: Business and Education Working Together* (Ottawa: Conference Board of Canada, 1990); Porter, *Canada at the Crossroads*; Economic Council of Canada, *A Lot to Learn*; Canada, *Inventing Our Future: An Action Plan for Canada's Prosperity* (Ottawa: Steering Group on Prosperity, 1992); Conference Board of Canada, *Dropping Out*; Canadian Labour Market and Productivity Centre, *Canada: Meeting the Challenge of Change: A Statement by the Economic Restructuring Committee*, Ottawa, 1993; New Brunswick, *To Live and Learn: The Challenge of Education and Training*, Report of the Commission on Excellence in Education, Fredericton, N.B., 1993; Ontario, *For the Love of Learning*, Report of the Royal Commission on Learning (Toronto: Queen's Printer for Ontario, 1994); Canadian Labour Force Development Board, *Putting the Pieces Together*.
5 Philip Nagy, "The Canadian Debate on National Standards," *Educational Leadership International*, supplement to *Educational Leadership* 52,6 (March 1995), pp.10-14.
6 Conference Board of Canada, *Employability Skills Profile*, Ottawa, 1992.
7 For detailed arguments, see Thomas Schweitzer, *The State of Education in Canada* (Montreal: The Institute for Research on Public Policy, 1995); and Stephen B. Lawton, *Busting Bureaucracy to Reclaim Our Schools* (Montreal: The Institute for Research on Public Policy, 1995).
8 Tanner, Krahn, and Hartnagel, *Fractured Transitions.*
9 For a review of the literature on this research see Harvey Krahn, *School-Work Transitions: Changing Patterns and Research Needs* (Ottawa: Human Resources Development Canada, 1996).
10 See Tanner, Krahn, and Hartnagel, *Fractured Transitions*, especially the final chapter, for a discussion of ways to reduce dropout rates.
11 Ontario Royal Commission on Learning, *For the Love of Learning: A Short Version* (Toronto: Queen's Printer for Ontario, 1994), p.12; see chapter 7 of the complete report for a review of the evidence on early childhood education.
12 See Rodney Haddow and Andrew Sharpe, eds., *Social Partnerships for Training: Canada's Experiment with Labour Force Development Boards* (Ottawa and Kingston: Caledon Institute of Social Policy and the School of Policy Studies, Queen's University, 1997).
13 Human Resources Development Canada, *Evaluation of the Co-operative Education Option: Summary Report*, Program Evaluation Branch, HRDC, Ottawa, 1994.

14 Ibid.
15 J. Darch, "Labour Market Outcomes for University Co-op Graduates," *Perspectives on Labour and Income*, Statistics Canada, Catalogue 75-001, 1995, pp.20-24.
16 See the discussion of apprenticeship in Economic Council of Canada, *A Lot to Learn*.
17 This is one area in which there is a good supply of research. See S. Conger, B. Hiebert, and E. Hong-Farrell, *Career and Employment Counselling in Canada* (Ottawa: Canadian Labour Force Development Board, 1994); Canadian Labour Force Development Board, *Putting the Pieces Together*; and OECD, *Mapping the Future*.
18 Conger, Hiebert, and Hong-Farrell, *Career and Employment Counselling*.
19 G. Betcherman, N. Leckie, and K. McMullen, *Developing Skills in the Canadian Workplace* (Ottawa: Canadian Policy Research Networks, 1997).
20 The training tax was one of the many issues that impeded efforts to promote "social partnership" in the development of the Ontario Training and Adjustment Board. See the cautionary tale by David Wolfe, "Institutional Limits to Labour Market Reform in Ontario: The Short Life and Rapid Demise of the Ontario Training and Adjustment Board," in Haddow and Sharpe, eds., *Social Partnerships for Training*.
21 See Betcherman, Leckie, and McMullen, *Developing Skills*, pp.82-83, for the discussion of the training problems of small employers and alternative approaches.
22 See G. Lowe and H. Krahn, "Job-Related Education and Training among Younger Workers," *Canadian Public Policy* 21,3 (September 1995). Lowe and Krahn's study showed that younger male workers received more workplace training than older workers, a finding at odds with other surveys. This may now be true of well-educated, young male workers in large firms.
23 J. DiNardo, N. Fortin, and T. Lemieux, "Labor Market Institutions and the Distribution of Wages, 1973-1992: A Semiparametric Approach," NBER Working Paper no. 5093.
24 See D. Card and A. Krueger, "Minimum Wages and Employment: A Case Study of the Fast Food Industry in New Jersey and Pennsylvania," *American Economic Review* 84 (1994), pp.772-93. The study is reported again in D. Card and A. Krueger, *Myth and Measurement: The New Economics of the Minimum Wage* (Princeton, N.J.: Princeton University Press, 1995).
25 M. Shannon and C. Beach, "Distributional Employment Effects of Ontario Minimum Wage Proposals: A Microdata Approach," *Canadian Public Policy* 21 (1994), pp.284-303.
26 M. Baker, D. Benjamin, and S. Stanger, "The Highs and Lows of the Minimum Wage Effect: A Time Series-Cross Section Study of the Canadian Law," University of Toronto Working Paper no. 9501.
27 The three studies are J-M Cousineau, D. Tessier, and F. Vaillancourt, "The Impact of the Ontario Minimum Wage on the Unemployment of Women and the Young in Ontario," *Relations Industrielles* 47 (1992), pp.559-66; T. Yuen, "The Effect of Minimum Wages on Youth Employment in Canada: Evidence from the Labour Market Activity Survey," unpublished manuscript, University of Toronto; and Baker, Benjamin, and Stanger, "Highs and Lows of the Minimum Wage Effect."
28 Organization for Economic Co-operation and Development, OECD *Jobs Study*, p.46.
29 Cited in Myles, "When Markets Fail," pp.116-40.
30 See, for example, Eric Shragge, ed., *Workfare: Ideology for a New Under-Class* (Toronto: Garamond Press, 1997).
31 See Giddens, *Beyond Left and Right*.
32 Madelaine Drohan, "Britain Weans Its Youth from State Benefits," *The Globe and Mail*, Jan. 8, 1998, p.A8.
33 Human Resources Development Canada, *Lessons Learned: Effectiveness of Employment-Related Programs for Youth*, Evaluation and Data Development (Ottawa: HRDC, 1997).
34 See C. Riddell, "Human Capital Formation in Canada: Recent Developments and Policy Responses," in *Labour Market Polarization and Social Policy Reform*, ed. K. Banting and C. Beach (Kingston, Ont: Queen's University School of Policy Studies, 1994), pp.123-67.

35 COMPAS Inc., *An Assessment of the Youth Initiatives Program: Surveys of Recent and Past Participants of the Youth Internship Canada and Youth Service Canada Programs* (Ottawa: HRDC, December 1997).

36 Gregory Albo, "'Competitive Austerity' and the Impasse of Capitalist Employment Policy," in *The Socialist Register 1994*, ed. Ralph Miliband and Leo Panitch (London: The Merlin Press, 1994), pp.144-70.

37 For details on Sweden's youth programs of the 1980s, see: Bjorn Jonson and Lois Recascino Wise, "Getting Young People to Work: An Evaluation of Swedish Youth Employment Policy," *International Labour Review* 128,3 (1989), pp.337-56; Graham Lowe, "Job Line for Youth," *Policy Options*, September 1986, pp.3-6; and Côté and Allahar, *Generation on Hold*, pp.152-58.

38 These figures are cited by Côté and Allahar, *Generation on Hold*, p.155. Even if they are inflated, the general point stands: this approach is very costly.

8 Conclusion: Social Solutions and Alternative Approaches

1 Cited in Albo, "'Competitive Austerity' and the Impasse of Capitalist Employment Policy."

2 Quoted in Jennifer Lewington, "The Higher Cost of Higher Education," *The Globe and Mail*, May 14, 1998, p.A4.

3 Robert E. Goodin and Julian Le Grand, *Not Only the Poor: The Middle Classes and the Welfare State* (London: Allen and Unwin, 1987), pp.97-101.

4 Margaret Philp, "Public Day Care Pays off for Whole Society, Study Says," *The Globe and Mail*, March 5, 1998, p.A8.

5 Jeremy Rifkin, *The End of Work* (New York: G. Putnam's Sons, 1996).

6 R. Morissette, J. Myles, and G. Picot. "Earnings Inequality and the Distribution of Working Time in Canada," *Canadian Business Economics* 2,3 (Spring 1994).

7 See Appendix IX of Human Resources Development Canada, *Report of the Advisory Group on Working Time and the Distribution of Work*, Ottawa, 1994.

8 See Swift, *Wheel of Fortune*; and Bruce O'Hara, *Working Harder Isn't Working: How We Can Save the Environment, the Economy and Our Sanity by Working Less and Enjoying Life More* (Vancouver: New Star Books, 1993).

9 See Human Resources Development Canada, *Report of the Advisory Group on Working Time*, for a full discussion of various means of redistributing working time.

10 For more discussion of the role the third sector could play in generating employment and creating valuable goods and services, see Lipietz, *Towards a New Economic Order*, pp.99-106; and Rifkin, *End of Work*, chapter 17.

Index

aboriginal youth, 23, 59, 76, 101, 119
adolescence, 31, 43
Alberta, 66, 76, 121, 122, 127-8
Alberta, University of, 68
Albo, Gregory, 133
Allahar, Anton, 99-100
Andres, Lesley, 62
Angus Reid polls, 6
anxiety, over labour market situation of youth, 4-5, 7, 27, 67, 112. *See also* moral panic
assortative mating, 105-6
apprenticeship: in preindustrial Hamilton, 17; in early industrial period, 20; decline of, 28, 63, 120; as alternative to high school completion, 61; in Germany, 64-5, 77, 120. *See also* youth apprenticeship
Asia, 44, 47, 112
Atlantic region, 4, 24, 25, 39, 53, 54, 128
Australia, 39

Axelrod, Paul, 22
baby-boom generation, 5, 43, 44, 47, 89
baby-busters, 5-6
Bancroft, Ontario, 1-2
Bank of Canada, 46
Barlow, Maude, 66-7
Beaudry, Paul, 91-2
Beck, Ulrich, 9
Bennett, Richard B., 31
Blair, Tony, 130
blue-collar occupations: employment in, 42, 49, 77-9, 82; unionization in, 85
Bourdieu, Pierre, 62
Bradbury, Bettina, 19-20
Britain, 34, 39, 46, 60-1, 130
British Columbia, 31, 76, 121, 122, 125, 127, 129-30, 134
British Columbia, University of, 68

Calgary, University of, 2, 68
Canada Pension Plan, 39, 126, 142, 144

Canadian Auto Workers, 85
Canadian Education Association, 42, 66
Canadian Federation of Students, 116
Canadian Manufacturers Association, 28
Canadian Opportunities Strategy, 116-7
Canadian Youth Commission, 37-8, 41-2
Career Edge, 119-20
Casino Windsor, 85
charter schools, 67, 113
child care, 57, 74, 105. *See also* early childhood education
child labour, 20-1, 25
Chrétien, Jean, 46, 69, 109
coming of age: milestones in, 7, 18; disorder in, 7, 13; changes in process of, 19, 31
Communist Party of Canada, 32, 97
community colleges, 2, 42, 61, 63-4, 68-9; employment and underemployment of graduates of, 78-9, 81; incidence of multiple jobs held by graduates of, 81; unemployment rates of graduates of, 75-6. *See also* education, postsecondary
Conference Board of Canada, 58, 86, 112
Contenta, Sandro, 60
Co-operative Commonwealth Federation (CCF), 38
co-operative education, 77, 111, 117-9
Côté, James, 99-100
Coulter, Rebecca Prieger, 32-3
Council of Ministers of Education, Canada (CMEC), 113
counselling (career, education, and employment), 51, 76, 77, 79, 121-2, 130, 134
Coupland, Douglas, 72
craft occupations, 15, 18, 19, 25, 28
credentialism, 49
cultural capital, 62, 101

Davis, Steven, 93

demography, as factor in labour market, 5-6
dependency, youth: prolongation of, 4, 18, 31, 72, 98-101
Depression, Great, 14, 31-33, 34, 37, 50, 97
disabled youth, 59, 76, 101
discouraged workers, youth as, 74
Dodge Report (1981) (Labour Market Development in the 1980s), 47
Dominion-Provincial Youth Training Programme, 32-3, 133
dropouts, 42, 53-4, 58-61, 74; and moral panic, 98; and streaming, 114; and student jobs, 73; and social class, 115; occupations of, 77-8; self-employment among, 81; unemployment rate of, 75;

early childhood education, 115, 140. *See also* child care; education
early leavers. *See* dropouts
earnings, labour market, 89-96. *See also* minimum wage
Economic Council of Canada, 45, 47
Edmonton, Alberta, 47, 55
education systems, 11, 14, 16, 21-4; denominational schools, 23, 113; elementary, 65, 66, 113-4, 138; postsecondary, 58, 61-3, 64, 67-9, 115-7, 118-9, 138-40; private, 24, 66-7, 69; secondary, 24, 27, 58-61, 65, 66, 113-4, 117-8, 120-1, 138 ; vocational, 27-31, 42, 63, 114. *See also* charter schools; early childhood education
education policy debates, 27-31, 65-67, 112-4
educational attainment: and earnings, 91-7, 154 n6; and employment, 77-9; and quality of work, 82-3; and underemployment, 79-81; and unemployment, 75-6; increasing levels of, among youth, 53-5; of young women, 56
Ehrenreich, Barbara, 10
Elmsley, John, 16
employer practices, 5, 44-6, 71-2, 94, 105, 137

employment, youth: multiple jobs, 81; part-time, 71-3, 80, 94; rates, 72-3; self-employment, 81, 131; summer, 73; temporary, 71, 80, 94
entrepreneurship training, 131, 143
Erikson, Erik H., 43
Esping-Andersen, Gosta, 39, 110
Europe, 21, 27, 44, 112; corporatist welfare states in, 39, 63; workplace training in, 122

family 14; and dropout rates, 59; changing structure of, 50; contribution of youth wages to, 19-20, 30-1, 72; importance of, during prolonged dependency, 97, 100-1
family wage, 26, 57
Finance, Department of, 46
Foot, David, 5-6
Forrester, Alexander, 21
free trade, 94, 111
full-employment policy, 38, 46

Gaskell, Jane, 29
gender differences: in career aspirations, 56-7, 102-4; in earnings, 90-6, 102; in education, 102; in hours worked, 93-4, 102; in life course patterns, 103-5; in occupations, 10, 77-9, 102; in underemployment, 79-81; in unpaid domestic labour, 102
gender relations, 102-7
Germany, 64-5, 77, 117, 120
Giddens, Anthony, 9
Gilbert, Sid, 59
Globe and Mail, The, 4, 105, 126-7
golden age, 14, 37, 39, 41, 72, 125
Goodin, Robert E, 139-40
Goodman, Paul, 43
Green, David, 91-2
guaranteed annual income. See negative income tax

Hall, G. Stanley, 31, 43
Hall-Dennis Report (1968), 66
Hamilton, Ontario, 15-19, 30-31, 43
Harris, Mike, 66, 67, 129

Heron, Craig, 20-1, 30-1, 146 n2
Hochschild, Arnie, 84
Holt, Derek, 89
human capital, theory of, 42, 62, 63, 64, 92, 125; human capital depletion, 86
Human Resources Development Canada (HRDC), 86-7, 119, 121-2

income-contingent repayment loans (ICRLs), 115-6, 139-40
income inequality: between age groups and generations, 89-96; between households, 106, 138; decline during golden age, 41; in United States, 128
industrial revolution 13, 14; Canadas first, 19-24; Canadas second, 24-35
internships, youth, 77, 111, 119-20

Japan, 44, 64, 122
job creation, 132-3, 142-3

Katz, Michael, 15-19
Keynes, John Maynard, 137
Keynesianism, 38, 44, 46, 47, 137
King, William Lyon Mackenzie, 32, 38
Klein, Ralph, 66, 67
Krahn, Harvey, 47-50

labour market: as source of security, 9-11, 34-5, 38, 106-7; primary, 39-40, 48-9, 85, 95; secondary, 39-40, 44, 48-9, 71; segmentation, 77, 148 n5; student, 71-4, 77, 78, 131; youth, 31, 39-41
labour-market training, 129-31
labour movement. See unions, labour
labour standards, 143-4
Latin America, 44, 47
Laval University, 68
Le Grand, Julian, 139-40
Licks Burger and Ice Cream Shops, 83
Limité (womens clothing shops), 85
literacy, 14, 86
Looker, E. Dianne, 56-7
Lowe, Graham, 47-50

Macdonald, John A., 38
Manitoba, 58, 119, 121
Manning, Preston, 109
manufacturing sector, employment in, 44, 49
Marchi, Sergio, 4
marginalized youth, 96-8
marriage: and dropping out, 59; and high divorce rate, 57, 103; as former bar to female labour market participation, 17, 26, 57; as career contingency, 56; as milestone in coming of age, 7, 13, 14, 18; as stabilizer of labour force participation of young men, 40; average age at, 15, 17, 31, 34, 50; detraditionalization of, 9, 50
Martin, Paul, 46, 69, 115
McDonalds restaurants, 85, 144
McGill University, 68
McJobs, 45, 48, 61, 85, 93, 127, 133; defined, 72
Mead, Margaret, 99
Mexico, 94
Millennium Fund, 69, 116-7, 125
minimum wage, 74, 93, 126-9
Montreal, 19
Montreal, University of, 68
moral panics, 97-8, 99
moratorium period, 43-4, 48; involuntary moratorium, 49
Mulroney, Brian, 46

Nagy, Philip, 112-3
National Policy, 38; Canadas Second, 38
negative income tax, 128-9
neo-liberalism, 46, 110, 116, 123, 128, 135, 137-8, 149 n21
New Brunswick, 131
New Zealand, 39
Newfoundland, 23, 53, 54, 58, 76,113
Non-Accelerating Inflation Rate of Unemployment (NAIRU), 46
North American Free Trade Agreement (NAFTA). See free trade
Northwest Territories, 121
Nova Scotia, 21, 32, 54, 56-7, 60, 68

Ontario, 21, 23, 24, 27, 31, 38, 66, 76, 121, 127-8, 129, 140
Ontario Royal Commission on Learning, 115, 140
Ontario Youth Apprenticeship Program (OYAP), 120-1
Organization for Economic Co-operation and Development (OECD), 65, 109-11, 128
Opportunities for Youth program, 132
Ottawa, Ontario 2, 21, 69, 97

Pan-Canadian Education Indicators Program (PCEIP), 113
parenthood: and child care, 57; and dropping out, 59, 74; and withdrawal of young women from labour market, 56, 74; as career contingency, 56, 104; as milestone in coming of age, 7; as stabilizer of labour force participation of young men, 56; increase in single, 50
payroll taxes, 94, 126-9
Polanyi, Karl, 34-5
Porter, John, 63
poverty, youth, 19-20, 96-8
preindustrial Canada, 13, 14-19
Prentice, Alison, 23
primary sector, employment in, 45, 53, 54
Prince Edward Island, 58
professional and managerial occupations, employment in, 78, 82
public sector: employment in, 3, 41, 82, 85; unionization in, 85

Quebec, 4, 23, 24, 31, 58, 69, 122, 125, 134, 127-8
Quebec Pension Plan, 39, 126, 144
Queens University, 63, 68

Reagan, Ronald, 46
REAL Women, 107
Regina Manifesto (1933), 38
Registered Education Savings Plan, 116
relief camps, 31-2
risk, individualization of, 5, 9-10, 51,

64, 65; due to detraditionalization of marriage, 103, 106-7
Robertson, Heather-jane, 66-7
Royal Commission on Industrial Training and Technical Education (1909-1913), 27, 32
rural youth, 4, 14-5, 22, 25, 33, 53-4, 58, 101
Ryerson, Egerton, 21, 27

Saskatchewan, 31, 33, 38, 128
Scandinavia, 39
School Achievement Indicators Program (SAIP), 113
School Leavers Survey, 59
school-work transitions, 48, 111, 117-122
schooling. See education
scientific management, 25, 29, 43, 44, 148-9 n14; in service jobs, 83-5
service sector, employment in, 41, 45, 48, 71, 77-9, 82-6, 87
Sir Sanford Fleming College, 2
skills: loss of, in service work, 84-6; employability, 40, 65, 86, 92-3, 112-3. See also literacy
squeegee kids, 97
Starbucks Coffee, 85
Statistics Canada, 47, 57, 74, 80, 93, 106
Steedman, Mercedes, 25-6
Steelworkers Union, 85
student labour market. See labour market, student
Sudbury, Ontario, 47
suicide, 100
summer jobs, 73, 131
Suzy Shier (womens clothing shops), 85
Sweden, 93, 134

Tanner, Julian, 61
Taylor, Frederick, 25
Taylorism. See scientific management
Teamsters Union, 85
technical occupations, employment in, 78, 82
telework, 83, 131
Thatcher, Margaret, 46, 66, 69, 116

third-sector enterprise, 143
Toronto, 16, 47
Toronto, University of, 68
training. See workplace training, labour-market training.
Tri-City study, 47-50, 55
tuition fees, postsecondary, 62, 64, 65, 67-9, 73, 101, 115-7, 125, 139-40

underemployment, youth, 4, 49, 79-81, 97
unemployment, youth, 4, 47, 49, 74-7, 94
United Nations Educational, Scientific, and Cultural Organization (UNESCO), 65
Union of Needletrades, Industrial, and Textile Employees (UNITE), 85
unions, labour, 14, 38, 41, 44, 85-6, 93, 144
United Food and Commercial Workers (UFCW), 85
United States, 21, 27, 39, 46, 63, 68, 94, 96, 122, 128; corporations, 24-5, 44.
universities, 2-3, 24, 38, 42, 67-9, 99; co-op programs, 118-9; earnings of graduates of, 91-2, 154 n6; employment and underemployment of graduates of, 78-9, 81; incidence of multiple jobs held by graduates of, 81; unemployment rates of graduates of, 75-6. See also education, postsecondary; tuition fees

Vancouver, B.C., 62
visible minorities, youth of, 76, 101

wages. See earnings
Wal-Mart, 85, 144
Wartime Emergency Training Programme, 33
Waterloo, University of, 68
Webber, Marlene, 98
Weir, H.A., 32
welfare state, 9, 14, 35, 38, 41, 46, 63, 110-1, 133-4; types, 39

Western Ontario, University of, 68
  Whyte, William, 43
  Willis, Paul, 60
  workfare, 129-30, 142-3
  working time: polarization of 93-6;
    redistribution of 140-2
  workplace training, entry-level, 122-3

World Trade Organization, 94
World War II, 14, 33-4, 38, 97
youth, definition of, 7
youth apprenticeships, 77, 111, 120-1
Youth Internship Canada, 119
youth, rural. *See* rural youth
Youth Service Canada (YSC), 132-3

S.S.F.C.
RESOURCES
CENTRE

174051